INTRODUCTION
TO BUDGETING

INTRODUCTION

TO BUDGETING

John Wanat UNIVERSITY OF KENTUCKY

Duxbury Press, North Scituate, Massachusetts

Library of Congress Cataloging in Publication Data
Wanat, John.
Introduction to budgeting.
Includes bibliographies and index.
1.   Budget.   2.   Government spending policy.   I.   Title.
HJ2009.W35   350'.722   77–14937
ISBN 0–87872–149–5
Duxbury Press
A Division of Wadsworth Publishing Company, Inc.

Introduction to Budgeting was edited and prepared for composition by Sylvia Stein. Interior design
was provided by Kathy Nitchie and the cover was designed by Oliver Kline.

L.C. Cat. Card No.: 77–14937
ISBN 0–87872–149–5
Printed in the United States of America
1 2 3 4 5 6 7 8 9—82 81 80 79 78

CODE
EEG3000

TITLE
INTRODUCTION TO BUDGETING

QUANTITY
39F19   1

TYPE   SOURCE   DATE   DEPOSITORY
20   1   1406   5/19/78   02   FC- 614953

For Susan and Sarah

CONTENTS

PREFACE

While everyone knows how a bill becomes a law, how a case gets to the Supreme Court, and how a person is elected president, few know how money is distributed in and by government. This book is a comprehensive and up-to-date presentation of the government spending process through an exposition of what budgets are, how they are made, how they are passed, and who is involved in them in what way.

This book is an introduction to the whole of budgeting. Therefore it is not a detailed how-to-do-it book, although there are many budget mechanics in it. Yet it is not a purely political explication or a grand theory book, even though those topics are amply covered. It is intended to be clear enough for the intelligent lay reader but still have enough substance to attract the attention of the public administration specialist.

Introduction to Budgeting is intended to serve five purposes. First, it can serve as a core text in any budget course. When that course is at the undergraduate level, the book, with a few additional readings, would be the basic text. In a graduate course this book would provide the skeleton upon which instructors could tailor classes to meet the specific configuration of their students' needs.

Second, in general public administration courses in which the instructor avoids a major text and assigns shorter topical books, this work could be used to cover the mandatory section on budgeting. It could also serve as a supplemental reading in conjunction with a major text.

Third, in public finance courses this book could supplement most texts because it emphasizes the political and behavioral aspects of government spending not always covered by most economists writing public finance books.

Fourth, for courses in government institutions this book provides a study of legislative-executive relations in a crucial area.

Last, this effort should satisfy the needs of the general reader interested in a vital aspect of government: spending tax money.

ACKNOWLEDGMENTS

While the actual writing of a book is a solitary endeavor, it cannot be done without the influence and assistance of others. I owe much to my wife Susan and my daughter Sarah. I am also endebted to the people who read and commented on various drafts. Ron Carson, Ronald Johnson, Jeffrey Straussman, and especially John Gist made helpful comments. Katharine Gregg, Sylvia Stein, Patrick Fitzgerald, and Robert Gormley at Duxbury Press all assisted in the production of the book. I am grateful to James Wilson who, in the birthplace of barbed wire, introduced me to budgeting. He and all the others, who have influenced and still affect my thinking, share whatever praise this book deserves.

INTRODUCTION TO BUDGETING

Chapter I

BUDGETING:

An Introduction

I n writing nonfiction it is customary for the author to begin by explaining to the reader why the book in hand is important or, lacking that, interesting. Writers covering such topics as nuclear energy, the population explosion, sexual techniques, and diets have a rather easy time in this endeavor. Even in the general area of government and politics, the nonfiction writer can usually rely on a certain residual interest held by most people. Consequently it takes little to convince the average public-spirited reader that it is worthwhile to read a book about how the Supreme Court makes momentous decisions, how lobby groups influence congresspersons, how candidates plot their elections, or how presidents grapple with questions of war and peace.

WHY STUDY BUDGETING?

Unfortunately the average reader's patience and interest does not often extend to the seemingly dull process of making and passing budgets. What follows is the traditional attempt to make clear why the apparently dry topic of budgeting is worth investigating. It is hoped that reading the next few pages will ensnare the reader.

In the last few years budgets have been more prominently discussed in the halls of government and the pages of the newspapers than in times past. New York City's financial straits in the mid-1970s consumed much of politicians' and bureaucrats' resources and claimed many columns of newspaper print. The size of the deficit in the federal budget has become a continuing focus of much political rhetoric and the continuation of many government programs normally taken for granted is now regarded as problematical. All of this attention to matters of public finance has become more salient with the decline of the economy in the 1970s. People are now, more than before, asking where money is coming from and, more important, where it is going. Periods of economic stringency heighten interest in budgets, which are commonly viewed as the plans or guidelines for government spending. But even before this new salience, budgets have deserved attention. In what follows six reasons are advanced for the importance of budgets and the interest that the general reader might show in them.

BUDGET SIZE

Most people are conversant with the concept of the Gross National Product, the GNP. This notion captures the economic activity of a society and can be defined as the sum total of the value of all goods and services produced in any nation. The GNP of the United States is generally over a trillion dollars. The size of the federal government's budget in 1976 was approximately $400 billion. The budget therefore was responsible for allocating the expenditure of a sizable proportion of all that is produced in this country. The mere size of the federal budget therefore makes it worthy of attention. Adding money from state and local budgets further heightens the impact of budgets and money on the economy.

Viewed from a historical perspective, the budgets of governments also bear watching. Over time, the fraction of the GNP that government budgets comprises has steadily risen. There is much comment made about the growing size of government and the declining role of the private sector. Whether one views this increased role of government in society with alarm or with pleasure, analysis of the budget provides an opportunity to monitor the phenomenon of governmental expansion.

POLICY PRIORITIES

In any government more elaborate than a small direct democracy there must be delegation. Citizens delegate their lawmaking powers to elected legislators. Lawmakers delegate the implementation of the laws they pass to the executive branch, where there is further delegation of policy implementation from the highest levels down to the most obscure civil servant. To the dismay of most, there is a suspicion that the megalith of government is at least partially out of control, each unit carrying out and elaborating the mandate delegated to it without any coordination with other units. The prevalent image is one of bureaucracy run wild, each agency doing its own thing.

To compound this fragmented governmental system, there is evidence that the legislature with its well-established committee system furthers the fragmentation of public policy. Legislators receive benefits for their constituents from particular agencies and consequently are eager for those agencies to expand. Public policy in this pluralistic governmental system is not easily amenable to any kind of centralized coordination from the legislatures, given the roles that most legislators must play to stay in office.

How then are priorities set among the myriad programs initiated by the legislatures? Each year, recently, over five hundred federal public laws are enacted, very few of which are passed with an eye to weaving a coherent tapestry of government programs. How then are priorities set among programs? Perhaps more basically, how can one keep track of all of the programs and,

in some centralized fashion, measure the relative commitment of the government to various programs? A government budget allows one to do this.

The one place where responsibility for coordination of policy is possible
is the chief executive's office. In recent times the executive branch has become
the major source of legislation and the legislatures have become the locus of
discussion, analysis, and approval of ideas usually originating elsewhere. Chief
executives' ideas and initiatives for policies can be modified by the legislature
and their priorities changed. But however the priorities in programs are initiated, chief executives must implement them — and implementation takes
money. To implement all programs, chief executives prepare their budgets,
their proposals for funding programs. The level of funding they propose indicates their priorities, and the modifications in their budgets made by the legislators indicate their priorities. This completed process is the closest thing found
in any pluralistic government to a statement of national priorities.

ACCOUNTABILITY

As previously mentioned, in every but the most primitive governments there
is some delegation of power and responsibility. When a legislator or chief
executive is elected, the citizenry delegates powers over themselves to those
elected officials. But the populace holds the officials responsible to them. In
basic democratic theory, the elected officials are held accountable by the threat
of not being reelected. As everyone quickly comprehends, the incentive of
reelection is a rather crude instrument by which to ensure accountability, primarily because the citizenry is generally ignorant of what the officials have done.
In the case of legislators, the citizen can examine a voting record; but although
a chief executive officer may initiate legislative proposals, the parentage of
statutes is not always clear. However, the set of priorities and proposals embodied in the budget prepared by the chief executive does allow a voter to compare
what the executive promised to do and what he or she tried to do. Thus the
budget can act as a means of holding at least the chief executive officer
accountable.

In an era of suspicions of government and its officials, citizens need a means
of accountability. But another form of accountability must be mentioned: the
accountability of the appointed civil service to the elected chief executive
and legislators. With a civilian federal bureaucracy of nearly three million
employees engaged in an enormous number of programs, how does one ensure
the responsiveness of these employees to legislative and popular desires? They

are not subject to periodic elections and in reality enjoy practically guaranteed job security. Once again the budget process offers a mechanism for overseeing executive branch operation.

In most governments each agency annually appears before its legislature's appropriations committees in order to receive money for its operation in the next year. At those hearings the agencies' top personnel justify what they want from the legislature by presenting material documenting their accomplishments in the past and stating what they hope to achieve in the next year. This legislative oversight of executive branch operation through the budget process is the only regular, routinized, and systematic means of gathering information by which the agency-level personnel can be held accountable to the elected officials in the legislature and, through them, to the populace at large.

DECISION MAKING

The three rationales just presented for investigating the budgetary process all appeal to interests in democracy, citizens' control over their government, and, more generally, citizen-regime relations. Thus, the concerned citizen in all of us would find budgets of some interest. But budgets have a more narrow appeal to academics, particularly social scientists, who have been very interested in decision making.

Decisions made by public officials obviously have an impact on all in society. Who makes the decisions, how they are made, and why they are made are all questions that have entranced or at least engaged the interests of political scientists. At least early on, the primary way in which government decisions were analyzed was by use of the case study. There are a plethora of case studies on important topics such as the civil rights laws, higher education assistance laws, campaign finance laws, Supreme Court decisions, presidential decisions in times of international conflict, and lobbying by important powerful trade associations, to name but a few. While studies such as these are usually in-depth analyses, they suffer from their idiosyncratic nature. What one learns about presidential decision making in the Cuban missile crisis may not be of much use in understanding presidential decision making in vetoing day care support legislation. Because legislatures do not pass redundant statutes, because courts do not rehear the same case, and because presidents do not get the chance to negotiate the same treaties over again, case studies can go only so far in illuminating government decision making.

For generalizable information on decision making by government officials the researcher must have repetitive decisions involving a relatively fixed set of actors under rather stable environmental conditions. The annual budget process satisfies all those requirements. Every year important decisions must be made about funding for all government programs. Since the programs usually persist, the "same" decision is considered year after year. The actors involved in this process are relatively fixed at the program and agency levels. The same congressional committee members generally meet the same executive branch personnel to consider the same or similar agency programs year after year. While there is a great degree of stability in this decisional process, changes do occur. There are shifts in the partisan configuration of the White House and the Capitol; there are changes in the aggressiveness with which agencies pursue their funding; new personnel appear on agency staffs; and, of course, new programs are occasionally advanced. But given the great variety and number of agencies, there are enough cases for the analyst to compare systematically the impact of differences in, say, agency acquisitiveness on final congressional committee decisions.

Many of the important questions raised by scholars of decision making can thus be analyzed in the budget process. The influence of information, time constraints, partisanship, coalitions, ideology, institutional arrangements, and many other factors on budget decisions are amenable to behavioral research because, to consider only one source, public documents are available from which variables such as those listed above can be operationalized. The findings regarding influences on decision making in the budgetary arena, while not generalizable to all decisional forums, give a solid basis for suggestions about how governmental figures make decisions.

INTRAGOVERNMENTAL RELATIONS

One of the more noticeable trends in politics over the last fifty or so years has been the expansion of the power and size of the executive at the expense of the legislative branch. The press of events in world affairs and domestic crises often requires quick action and almost always demands a level of technical expertise usually not found in legislatures. The role of the deliberative bodies has therefore been largely one of oversight. The quality of the oversight has been crucially important insofar as elected legislators are the one way average citizens think they can have some control over the ever-growing executive. Just how can the quality of this oversight, this aspect of legislative-executive relations, be gauged? As might be expected, the budgetary nexus provides a convenient as well as central opportunity.

The executive and the legislature interact in many forums. At the federal level, for instance, the president proposes nominations for various positions in government that the Senate must consider and hopefully approve. The executive branch negotiates treaties the Senate is called upon to ratify. The president proposes legislation and hopes the Congress will pass it. In many ways the president interacts with the Congress. All of those just mentioned would, if analyzed, give a somewhat biased and certainly a rather narrow picture of the relations between the two most salient branches of the federal government. The Senate, for example, rarely rejects treaties negotiated by the executive; but treaties are few in number and many contractlike arrangements with foreign powers are handled by executive agreement.

Because all executive branch activity requires money and because all monies must be approved by Congress, analysis of legislative-executive relations through the budget process allows an important look at a central relationship between the branches. The view afforded by the budget perspective is extensive in covering almost all agencies and is intensive inasmuch as there is occasional congressional investigation of lower level agency operations.

Not only does the budget allow examination of relations between legislatures and executive agencies, it also allows some analysis of relations among various executive branch organizations. Since 1921 at the federal level, agencies seeking money from Congress must have their requests approved by the president through what is now named the Office of Management and Budget (OMB). Before the cabinet agency request gets to OMB, it is usually examined by the intermediate department-level budget office. Thus the interaction of agency, department, and budget office can be measured in hard dollar terms and appropriate inferences made about how subunits of the executive branch relate to one another.

PRACTITIONERS' NEEDS

Lastly, it is important to study budgets because budgets must be prepared. Agencies must formulate plans of activity for the upcoming year to seek funding for those activities. The materials that elaborate the programs, objects, and activities that must be purchased are found in the budget document itself. This document is important for the executive branch managers to plan their activities. It is important for the higher echelon executives to coordinate and to decide upon funding levels for the competing programs. It is necessary for the legislative oversight personnel who must decide how much money to appropriate.

As one might easily imagine, the way requests are made might have an effect on the final disposition of the requests as well as influencing how the managerial problems are handled. There are myriad budget formats, each tailored to or the consequence of unique historical, political, and managerial needs and demands. Those entering public service as well as those already in it need some familiarity with the mechanics of budgets and budgeting to understand and to operate in an environment where the budget is a crucial annual event.

THE MANY FACETS OF BUDGETING

If budgeting is of interest because of all the reasons above, it obviously is a many-faceted phenomenon. Indeed, it is a Roshomon-like phenomenon, meaning different things to different people. Budgeting can be viewed from at least the following seven perspectives:

as an allocation mechanism whereby a significant proportion of the nation's resources are channeled into efforts decided upon in the governmental sector

as a process that organizes the appropriation of money by elected leaders for specific purposes

as a stylized interaction among groups of governmental elites, all of whom have specific interests, stakes, and motivations for seeing particular budgetary outcomes

as a technical tool for controlling expenditures, for managing agencies, for planning programs

as a ritual in which many political and governmental figures go through the paces leading to a nearly foreordained conclusion

as plain and simple politics, by which is meant "who gets what, when, and how"

as a measurement of certain outputs of the governmental system

While each of these perspectives may appeal in differing degree to each reader, to understand the phenomenon of budgeting one must understand all of them. To that end this book is organized with a chapter covering each of those perspectives in order. For those who wish to read only those portions of the book that are most germane to their interests, the following suggestions are made.

To those who have a pragmatic and perhaps economic orientation, most probably those who are practitioners or who are soon to be practitioners, chapters 2, 3, 5, and 8 would be of special interest. To the general reader of politics who seeks institutional description of the budget process, chapters 3, 4, and 5 should be read first. For the general student of politics who wishes to see how politics operates in the budgetary process, chapters 4, 6, 7, and 8 would be of the most utility.

SUMMARY

Budgeting is worth studying for a number of reasons. First, the impact of government on the economy can be assessed by the magnitude and composition of government spending as presented in budgets. Second, the priorities among programs set by governmental elites are manifested in budgets. Third, budgets provide information on governmental activity that is necessary for the responsible citizen to review intelligently the actions of the government administration. Budgets also provide information needed by legislators to carry out their duties of overseeing the bureaucracy. Fourth, analysts of decision making find in the budget process an excellent "laboratory" for the investigation of government decisions because of the stability of the participants, the similarity of the problems, and the regularity of the procedures. Fifth, because the formulation and execution of the budget takes place in the executive branch while the approval and some of the review occurs in the legislative branch, the budget process offers an excellent arena in which to examine legislative-executive relations. Sixth, budgeting is worth studying because government employees must prepare, defend, approve, and execute budgets in the course of their duties.

Chapter II

BUDGETS AS ALLOCATORS:

A Necessity

Contemporary life is collective life. Like it or not, interdependence characterizes the lot of a person in society today. No longer is it possible for a person to live the ideal of the Jeffersonian yeoman, sufficient unto himself. The closest approximation to self-sufficiency today is the farmer, whose numbers have steadily shrunk since the founding of this country. Even the less than 5 percent of the population classified as farmers, however, are highly dependent on others for markets, for subsidies, for specialized equipment, for fertilizers, and for most common commodities. Most people are at the mercy of great numbers of other people, largely unknown and unseen. The chaos the entire nation is thrown into by a strike in most industries clearly illustrates this point.

The collective nature of contemporary society arises because people need and desire things and services beyond their skills and resources to produce. Because of particular capabilities possessed by some and because of the need for efficient production, specialization of labor and specialization of production emerged. When one grows one's own food, builds one's own house, weaves one's own clothes, and so on, there is no need to rely on others. What is needed is produced. But when the producers are not the consumers, there is no guarantee that what is needed will be produced nor is there any guarantee that what is produced is needed. This gives rise to a major problem of collective life: How can the resources of society be allocated so that there is maximal utility for the producers, the consumers, and the society as a whole?

This general problem is seen more clearly in specific instances. Given a pool of labor in society, how many workers should be allocated to police, to medicine, to law, and so on? Given the supply of petroleum products available, how much oil should be allocated to recreational use, to defense vehicles, to mass transit, or to any other use that can be imagined? In any collectivity so large that members cannot recognize each other on sight, there must be some more or less automatic mechanism that determines how much shall be produced of each scarce service and good and that also determines who shall be able to receive how much of each scarce service and good.

ALLOCATION MECHANISMS

In general there are two allocation mechanisms found in modern societies: the market or free enterprise mechanism and the central command mechanism. Both usually operate to some degree in all societies. In some nations, however, the proportion of resources that are allocated by a command decision from some central governmental power center is far greater than in others. Those nations that rely heavily on a central command allocation mechanism are usually more socialist and those that rely more heavily on the market allocation system more capitalist. Governmental activity, however, is always associated closely with the command system and its details are manifested through a budget. Since our interest lies in budgets, attention will be paid to the command system. But to understand that mechanism, we will compare it with its rival allocation system. Before the advantages and disadvantages of each system are considered, a brief description of both mechanisms is in order.

MARKET OR FREE ENTERPRISE SYSTEM

Conceive of a modern society as a collection of people each producing some good or providing some service. Thus there is a panoply theoretically available to everyone. Each person desires some relatively unique mixture of the goods and services theoretically available. Matching up the producers and the consumers is the problem that the marketplace generally handles in this society.

The **market*** or free enterprise system is an allocation system that operates impersonally, based on individual decisions, relying on price to provide divisible goods available on a quid pro quo basis. Its operation theoretically provides those goods desired by consumers in the quantities and at the prices fixed by the intensity and extensity of the consumers, by the supplies available to the producers, and by the prospect of financial gain for the producers. To give an illustration, if consumers desire smaller, more economical automobiles, cars on the market that are small and economical will sell quickly and larger expensive models will sit in dealers' showrooms. Producers, eager to make a profit and aware that small cars satisfy the consumers, will then procure the raw materials and process them to manufacture the more economical variety of automobile. Consumers thus find that whatever goods they want are available and producers find that the profit they seek is secured. Should the fickle desires of the consumers shift back to large, pretentious vehicles, they will buy fewer of the smaller automobiles and manufacturers' profits from those cars will fall. They understandably will then divert their productive capacity from the small cars to the bigger cars, where a profit is to be made.

Multiply this scenario by every type of service and commodity generally available and one can see how the desires of the consumers can be satisfied

* Throughout the book definitional terms are printed in boldface type in the text. The page citations for terms in the index are also in boldface type.

without any centralized process. The "hidden hand" of the market shifts scarce resources to those uses where the price is highest and where, presumably, the demand is greatest. The market's allocation of labor, supplies, and productive potential so as to maximize profit for the producer simultaneously provides the consumers with what they desire. At least that is what happens in theory.

CENTRAL COMMAND SYSTEM

The second model or mechanism for allocating the many resources in society to the many demands or needs is what this book calls the **command mechanism.** The market system is somewhat inaccurately portrayed as egalitarian or democratic because everyone's dollar is the same and the sheer weight of financial demand for some service will see to it that the demand is satisfied. On the other hand, the command system is depicted as being more elitist, more authoritarian, and potentially more inequitable. Under this mechanism individual preferences for goods and services are not directly registered with the producers. Instead, for resources to be allocated to a particular use those possessing power or the ability to coerce have the final decision. Such a decision is usually not made in the impersonal manner of the market but generally in a highly personal manner with particular attention paid to who seeks the good or service. Briefly, those having power extract resources from others and then decide the purposes to which the resources are to be applied and, inevitably, the beneficiaries of the resource allocation.

Under the command allocation system, the mechanism typically associated with governments, there is no clear-cut and universally applicable set of rules, motivations of the participants, or tactics utilized by those allocating resources. It therefore is much more difficult to describe in general terms. But it can be seen in some detail through the process of budgeting.

WHY A COMMAND ALLOCATION SYSTEM?

Based on the brief description of the two allocation mechanisms, it seems hard to see why the command allocation system would be employed. It, after all, is possibly nondemocratic, it certainly employs coercive power, and it can operate in a nonresponsive manner, to name but a few of its more objectionable characteristics. To get down to basic realities, the real question is why have government allocate resources, or, more generally, why have government? Two general responses will be made to justify the existence of command allocation through the medium of budgets. The first rationale relies on the failure of the market system in certain areas and the second rationale refers to the obligation of government to provide positive initiative to "better" its citizenry and to further the commonweal. Both of these sets of justifications have theoretical precedent in schools of political philosophy and their attempts to justify or explain the existence of government in society.

Thomas Hobbes, John Locke, and Jean Jacques Rousseau all theorize that government, or, more precisely, the governmental apparatus, exists as a result of some kind of contract between the citizens and the rulers, the Leviathan, in Hobbes's terms. Citizens realize that there are certain protections, guarantees, and services that they as individuals cannot provide for themselves. They consequently create a superordinate body, the government, to which they contract out for the protections and services they desire. In return for those goods, they offer support for the regime by accepting its directives and providing resources to the government, which are used to protect and serve the populace. This overly simplified version of the contract theorists' political philosophy serves as a prototypical explanation for the substitution of the market allocation system by the command budget system.

In the market system the individual consumer "contracts" with a producer for a specified good at a particular price agreeable to both buyer and seller. Individuals thereby receive something they are incapable or unwilling to provide for themselves. However, there are certain goods and services the market cannot, will not, or is reluctant to provide. Because of the market's failure in certain circumstances, government steps in to provide the needed goods and services by commandeering resources, usually through taxation, and by redistributing them to the purposes deemed appropriate by those governing. In what follows, the inadequacies of the market are presented in four situations.[1] The only alternative left in each of these four situations is for command allocation of resources, that is to say, for allocation through some budget process.

FAILURE TO PROVIDE COLLECTIVE GOODS

First, the market or free enterprise system fails to provide society with what are termed **collective goods.** These are generally services that are not sufficiently divisible so that a person paying for the services gets the services and a person not paying does not benefit from the service. To give examples, everyone would like to be secure from aggression from alien powers, to be protected from fire, to have police protection, to have someone conduct relations with foreign countries, and to enjoy an equitable judicial system. But, to focus on one example, if an army, navy, and air force are maintained, everyone benefits from the military presence whether or not everyone pays for it or even expressly asks for it. Were military services provided through some kind of market system, individuals would contract for, say, a year's worth of antiballistic missile protection and would pay some price. But anyone in the country not desiring or not paying for the protection would still have the protection. This problem of the free-rider is not easily soluble in the market. One might, for example, pay a fixed amount to a local police organization for a guarantee of a dozen police calls, but even were that approximation to a market quid pro quo operative, people not subscribing to the police service would still benefit from the general deterrent effect of some kind of police presence.

The indivisibility characteristic of a number of services demanded by the general populace makes provision of those services inappropriate through the market mechanism. Since national defense, diplomatic representation, and a police system, to name but a few of these services, must be provided in order for a society to survive, their provision falls by default to the command allocation system. In other words, money must be extracted from all beneficiaries, whether they want to contribute or not, and funneled into specified purposes by those in the government given the responsibility to maintain the society. This allocation takes place through the budget process.

FAILURE TO PROVIDE CERTAIN SERVICES

A second defect in the market lies in its inability to provide services efficiently where price does not indicate the true worth of the services. Situations such as these, often called **diseconomies** or **external economies,** can be illustrated in the area of education. A student pursuing, say, a college education pays tuition to his or her school. That tuition does not measure accurately the value of the college education. There are intangible benefits that accrue to the student, such as perception, perspective, and appreciation of fine arts, which no price tag can accurately measure. There are also tangible benefits, such as the increased earning potential of a college-educated student over a high school diploma holder. But even in the area of the tangibles, the price paid in tuition does not easily measure the monetary value of the training. The tuition paid by a law student and a graduate student in literature is the same, while the value of a J.D. degree in future earnings far exceeds the monetary value of a Ph.D. in English.

To shift attention from benefits received by the direct recipient of an education, consider the benefit society as a whole receives from a well-trained and educated citizenry. For example, even though medical students pay a small amount for a valuable education that guarantees them large incomes throughout life, society theoretically enjoys access to trained personnel who can try to cure what ails people. A healthy society is desired and its monetary value cannot be measured by the tuition payments made by the student.

Because a dollar figure cannot precisely measure the value of literacy to either the literate or to society as a whole, the market, which relies on price to direct resources to meet demands, is less than adequate. A command decision is consequently made that money shall be devoted to education to pay for it totally, as at the primary and secondary school level, or partially, as at the collegiate and professional school levels.

FAILURE TO TAKE CERTAIN RISKS

A third arena where markets cannot efficiently allocate money to provide services needed by collective society involves extraordinary risks. The engine that drives the market is the expectation of profit. If the risks involved in investing resources in a venture are very high, it is unlikely that investors will allow their money to be allocated to such a venture, no matter how intrinsically important the venture may be to the well-being of society as a whole. The development of atomic energy, of various weapons systems, or of supersonic aircraft all provide recent examples of expenditures that required a large investment in a risky area. Yet it was crucial for the continued existence of the country over three decades ago to develop nuclear energy for military purposes and for electric energy production right now. Government used its coercive powers of taxation to gather the money, which was then directed by command decisions from key political and administrative figures into atomic energy research and development.

FAILURE TO FUNCTION IN NATURAL MONOPOLIES

The fourth set of circumstances of market inadequacy centers on what are called **natural monopolies.** Central to the notion of market allocation is the requirement of competition. In other words, there must be multiple suppliers of a commodity to ensure that only those providing a quality commodity will draw consumers to their product. Likewise there must be multiple buyers for any commodity or else the single purchaser can determine the price, quantity, and quality of the commodity desired.

There are certain services and goods that have only one buyer or that have only one producer. When dealing with those goods and services the market cannot operate well and an alternative mechanism must be employed. Since most of those goods and services are required to meet needs of society, government steps in to provide them through a command system, which is manifested through the budget process. Examples of goods and services best provided in a noncompetitive manner are utilities, mails, and defense. Obviously it makes little sense to have multiple sets of water mains or sewer pipes under the ground in a city because the capital investment would be prohibitively high for each utility provider. Therefore it is not likely for competition to an established utility to arise. Similarly when there is only one buyer for a commodity, such as an aircraft carrier, deemed necessary to the national defense, the competition usually expected to guarantee the proper quantity and quality of the commodity is lacking and the market cannot allocate efficiently.

"GOVERNMENT KNOWS BEST"

As mentioned earlier there is a second set of reasons why a command allocation system is needed to distribute resources for a collective body. Among political philosophers that foreshadow the second rationale are men such as Aristotle and Plato. For them the state is meant to provide a setting in which the individual can live a virtuous life. The government rules, in Plato's case, by a philosopher king, who knows what is best for the populace and who uses his position and the power behind his position to dedicate resources to whatever purposes he deems best for the society.

In more recent times other political philosophies have been supportive of regimes that took the position that the regime had the right and the obligation to do what is "best" for the populace, irrespective of what the people may have said they wanted. Fascist and communist regimes operate in this manner as do some of the one-party regimes found in developing countries. In these cases there is generally an ideology, a doctrine, a belief system that spells out the nature of the universe, of human beings, and of society; and it is this ideology that contains the priorities that government should follow. The regime then commands resources to be applied through a budget to the programs and priorities called for by the ideology.

Most Americans regard the doctrinaire regimes previously referred to as repugnant and allow that repugnance to color their attitude toward command allocation systems. This is partly because the political systems most often associated with command allocation mechanisms give priority to the state over the individual, whereas the American system at least in theory makes the state subordinate to the individual. It would be an incorrect inference, however, to say that the command allocation system is inextricably entwined with doctrinaire, authoritarian regimes and cannot or does not belong in a more democratic political system. Apart from reliance on a command system required by faults in a market system, democratic regimes need to utilize a command allocation system.

Although democracies are characterized as systems in which the government serves the people and not the reverse, because democracies are collective entities usually operating under some kind of majority rule provision, some people will inevitably be unhappy with the decisions made by the majority or the representatives of the majority. When a policy is decided upon by a majority of the people through their representatives, prohibition, for example, some people will not want to comply and the government has to devote resources to guarantee compliance. In effect, a popularly mandated goal initiates action requiring governmental utilization of its coercive powers. Government must command monetary resources to prevent, in this example, the manufacture and sale of alcoholic beverages. Command allocation of resources is needed to compel opinion minorities to conform to the majority decision.

In a related fashion persons may tell the government that it should pursue a particular policy but disagree with the implementation. For instance, a citizen may tell the government to reduce crime but may not like the intrusions into privacy that the law and order emphasis brings with it or may not like the increased efficiency in catching speeders (him or herself) brought on by the use of more sophisticated police equipment. In all such cases the government, once given a mandate or at least not being vetoed in its policy proposals, cannot rely on the stable goodwill of all the citizenry to comply with the mandate or policy. It must use its powers to command allocated resources. In other words budgets must be used to allocate money to programs and policies popularly chosen because people are neither consistent over time nor compliant with a majority opinion to contribute money voluntarily to programs and policies.

The point of the previous few paragraphs is that democratic regimes can responsively set priorities or establish "ideologies" that the government is to implement, even though some objection to those priorities will be made by some part of the political system. In the United States in particular there are some clearly perceivable policies and priorities given to government to implement. These policies exemplify what society considers to be needed to lead the good or virtuous life or at least not to lead a life of misery. Consider three policies that have been given to government to carry out: reduction of unemployment, regulation of antisocial and harmful behavior, and relief of poverty. These indicate that the "good" or "virtuous" life in this country would be one of continuous and prosperous employment, with behavior conforming to accepted norms, with no one being poor. We now examine government action in each area in a bit more detail.

In America work is considered a basic requirement for respectability. The puritan work ethic is deeply entrenched in most people's psyches and the unemployed suffer from blows to their self-esteem as well as to their wallets. People with jobs are considered responsible, respectable, and the ideal material from which a good citizen can evolve. Conversely, those without jobs can create a source of civil disturbance, urban turmoil, or crime. Since unemployment can arise and continue from causes outside the control of the individual, government has stepped in to reduce the undesirable situation of large-scale unemployment.

One landmark piece of legislation that clearly illustrates the federal government's commitment to an employed populace is the Employment Act of 1946. Stunned by the collapse of the economy in the 1930s and emboldened by Keynesian doctrines of governmental efficacy in influencing the economy, the federal government made it a public policy, that is to say a goal of the government, to reduce unemployment. Another instance of governmental commitment to the goal of full employment is the Emergency Employment Act that empowered the government to offer employment to those without jobs. Numerous statutes supporting job training and job retraining for those without marketable skills also illustrate this point.

Government also has been called on to prohibit people from engaging in self-destructive behavior. Just as a parent will not give a loaded firearm to a child as a toy, society thinks that it is in the interests of the individual and society as a whole to prevent people from or warn people about engaging in certain behavior. When certain segments of this country deemed that alcohol had effects that should not be tolerated and gained enough agreement from

the citizenry to pass a constitutional amendment, government was then called
in to enforce the norms of nondrinking good citizenship by using its powers
to prevent the manufacture and sale of alcoholic beverages. Similarly, when
linkages between smoking and various diseases, particularly lung cancer, became well known, in an attempt to protect the health of the populace, government felt it proper to commit its resources to informing people of the dangers
of smoking, to forbidding the advertising of cigarettes on television, and to
requiring warnings of the dangers of smoking to be placed on all cigarette
packages and in all advertisements. These two examples show how government
will use its resources to modify the behavior of the citizenry when government
considers behavior of the populace not to be in their own long term self-interest.
In situations like these it is obvious that there has to be authoritative allocation
of resources from some central point to attain the desired goals because individual and voluntary action would not be adequate.

A third area wherein government acts for the common good with support
in general but perhaps not in all particulars is in the reduction of poverty
through the augmentation of income. It is obviously not in the interest of the
society to have very many poor people, if for no other reason than because
poverty can lead to discontent of such depth that violence and civil strife
will ensue. In a less self-interested vein, however, a sense of empathy and
charity in most people leads to a desire to relieve poverty. In times gone past
assistance to the poor generally came from the extended family, churches,
and voluntary organizations. With the breakup of the extended family system,
the loss of importance of religious organizations, and the inability of private
charitable organizations to cope with the magnitude of the poverty problem,
government has felt obliged to attack the problem. Social Security, unemployment compensation, Supplemental Security Income, and Aid to Families with
Dependent Children are all indicative of governmental initiative in reducing
poverty.

In the three areas just considered, as well as in many more, authoritative
decisions are made about what is good for the society and steps are taken
to see to it that the goals are accomplished. The means whereby the ends
are achieved are governmental programs that are funded through the central
allocation process of formulating, approving, and executing a budget.

THE RELATION BETWEEN COMMAND AND MARKET SYSTEMS

Command and market allocation mechanisms were presented as polar opposites primarily for purposes of explanation. In reality there is considerable grey area where the two systems overlap. To give a few examples, private firms such as Pinkerton's provide police and protective services that are bound to have some spillover benefits to society in general. Even though there is a strong rationale for public provision of education, everyone knows that private educational institutions exist. And while natural monopolies are theoretically best administered by a public organization, they typically are provided by nongovernmental organizations whose rate structure and quality of services are supervised by public service commissions. There are even joint private firm and government ventures such as the communications satellite corporation, COMSAT, and the ill-fated supersonic transport program.

In spite of the twilight zone of overlap and similarity between the command and market allocation systems, it is generally possible to distinguish countries by their reliance on one or the other system. In countries like the USSR, China, Sweden, and Denmark there is heavy reliance on a command system to allocate societal resources. In the United States, Germany, the Philippines, Canada, and Japan there is major reliance on the market. The reason some countries follow one system more vigorously than the other often is based on ideology. Communist and most varieties of socialist countries hold that relying on the profit motive to distribute services and goods will not guarantee equitable provision to all people and they therefore use the command system to distribute at least basic necessities such as utilities, transportation, and food. These countries have a more or less explicit notion of what should be done for the people and usually have a governmental structure that is sufficiently unified that once goals are set they will be implemented.

In the more capitalist countries agreement on what should be done for or to the average citizen is less forthcoming and the governmental structure is generally more decentralized or fragmented. No one group of people can control enough of the authoritative centers of power consistently to implement what they desire. There is generally less dissatisfaction with how the market is distributing goods and services, perhaps because the capitalist countries have been more prosperous. There could, therefore, be more slippage and inefficiency in the allocation of such societies' wealth.

But, apart from any influence of ideology or wealth, there is a trend in all societies toward heavier utilization of the command allocation mechanism. The history of the United States gives ample evidence of this assertion. From a society that two hundred years ago was basically rural, agrarian, self-contained, and dominated by a laissez-faire philosophy, this country has developed into an urban, industrial, and highly interdependent society. With this shift there has been a strong call for more government.

Increasing population creates more occasions for conflict and hence the need for more adjudicatory mechanisms. Greater interdependence in the economy brought on by nationwide commerce brings on the need for uniformity of standards and operating procedures across jurisdictions. Increased responsibility in the international scene means more diplomatic representation and military presence. And the constant wave of heightened expectations formed in the citizenry puts greater demands on the government. All of these trends call for more government, which means more resources are diverted into the public sector. In that sector, it has been pointed out, decisions about where the money goes are made not through any market mechanism but through a command mechanism, that is to say, a political mechanism.

ADDITIONAL FUNCTIONS OF THE BUDGET

This chapter has emphasized the command system of budgeting as a means for allocating resources. Like most processes and phenomena in society, budgeting serves more than one function. As Musgrave points out, budgets serve not only to allocate resources, but also to stabilize the economy and to distribute income.[2] The magnitude of public spending alone guarantees government officials some leverage in changing the state of the economy. The source of government revenues as well as their destination also acts as a potentially powerful tool to redistribute wealth. The emphasis on budgets as allocators does not imply that their role as stabilizers or distributers is not important. For the purposes of this book, however, the allocation function is preeminent and so that aspect is emphasized.

POLITICS AND MONETARY ALLOCATIONS

So far in this chapter the rather abstract term command allocation system has been used in talking about how money is distributed in governments. But no clue has been given how this is done. This is largely because the process is basically politics and politics is not easily definable. If it were subject to nice, easily understandable, and mutually agreed-upon rules, budgetary allocations would be easily predictable. That, however, is not the way the political budgetary world works.

In the chapters that follow details will be presented that will allow the reader to understand in more detail the mechanism through which well over a quarter of this country's GNP is allocated. In the next chapter the sequence of events and the procedures utilized by which government distributes money will be related. This narrative will form the basis for the more political aspects that will be presented in succeeding chapters.

SUMMARY

Because people cannot provide all that they need for themselves, they must rely on others for many goods and services. In contemporary collective society the allocation of goods and services is provided through two mechanisms: the free market system and the command allocation system. Government allocates society's resources by commanding that taxes be collected and then by commanding where those taxes will be spent. This chapter examined why government must extract and distribute society's resources.

Command allocation is necessary in part because the market mechanism is not adequate. Services and goods that cannot be divided, or collective goods as they are called, will not be provided by a profit-driven market. Situations where price is not a good indicator of the value of a service also are not attractive to private firms. Similarly, goods and service provisions where extraordinary risks are involved will not find free enterprise operating. Finally, the case where natural monopolies occur, where only one producer of a good or service can reasonably operate, militates against the operation of a free market. Because goods and services would not be provided by the market in these situations, the government must use its coercive powers to command that certain resources be allocated in particular ways.

Government also allocates resources through the command system because people feel that it ought to pursue positive goals and not only remedy deficiencies in the market system. For example, government uses its coercive powers to command that monies be allocated to reduce unemployment, to relieve poverty, and to discourage antisocial behavior because the populace wants those things to be done.

The most immediate means by which government at any level and in any country command allocates financial resources is through the budget process.

NOTES

1. The organization and treatment of the need for budget allocation of resources in the rest of this chapter draws on the presentation made by Otto Eckstein, *Public Finance* (Englewood Cliffs, N.J.: Prentice-Hall, Inc., 1964), pp. 10–17.

2. Richard A. Musgrave, *The Theory of Public Finance* (New York: McGraw-Hill, 1959).

SELECTED BIBLIOGRAPHY

Practically any introductory work on public finance, such as those cited above, will cover the matters addressed in this chapter.

Chapter III

BUDGETS AS PROCESS:

The Budget Chronology

A basic, if not the most basic, problem in any democratic political system is ensuring responsiveness of the government to the populace. Particularly with regard to those goods and services uniquely provided by government the question is how can one be sure that those in positions of power provide what the citizenry desires. As the last chapter indicated, governmental or command allocation of resources has the potential for much abuse. Unlike a perfect and so a constantly adjusting market mechanism, command allocation has no intrinsically equilibrating dynamic.

In the purely theoretical realm, responsiveness of a political system is approximated in a representative democracy by the periodic election of crucial personnel in government. The lack of responsiveness associated with dictatorships is partly attributable to the permanency of the dictator's control over the governmental apparatus. If those serving in a political system are subject to review of their stewardship occasioned by periodic election, the theory says that those representatives who do not satisfy the desires of the electorate will be replaced by those who will, or who at least promise to do so. Because voters do not always know what their elected officials are doing or have done, this mechanism does not always engender responsive government. Additionally, because much governmental decision making is made by people not subject to reelection, the bureaucrats, actions taken by government are not always responsive to the desires, however wise or foolish, of the populace.

The crucial characteristic of representative democracy for control purposes, then, is periodic popular evaluation of the regime's performance. In the more specific area of the command allocation of resources the same periodic evaluation therefore needs to be employed. Especially since the overwhelming proportion of those involved in distributing government resources through the budgetary process are not elected to office, there must be periodic oversight of their activity. Controlling the money available to government largely controls what it does and how it does it. The periodic process by which money is allocated is the subject of this chapter.

THE BUDGET CYCLE

The need for representativeness and accountability has been presented as the motivation or rationale for periodic review of how resources are allocated by government. The notions of representation and accountability immediately raise the questions of "representative of what" and "accountable to whom."[1] In democratic governments the populace at large is ultimately the body to which the governmental apparatus is accountable. However, the general public is rarely involved in the budgetary process. In its place the elected legislators — be they congresspersons, members of the state general assembly, or municipal council members — are supposed to be the counter or the foil to the largely nonelective executive branch, which seeks to allocate money. In what follows the tensions between the legislative and executive branches of governments will be used as the vehicle to describe and explain the phases of the **budget cycle.**

To understand the tensions and counterbalancing between legislatures and executives today, consider the composition of the two branches and their differing functions. In most jurisdictions the executive branch is generally composed of scores of formal bureaucracies. Bureaucracy is a form of organization that is, among other attributes, characterized by specialization of knowledge, expertise, and a hierarchy of authority that coordinates the diverse yet highly skilled personnel of the organization to attain the goals set out for it. Government bureaucracy, moreover, is generally quite large, so large that impersonal and written rules of operation guide the activity of those in the executive branch. A major advantage of this form of organization lies in its ability to divide a problem into manageable components, which are then mastered by the pertinent experts. The nineteenth-century sociologist, Max Weber, in fact, considered bureaucracy the most efficient form of organization available.

In legislatures there is only rudimentary specialization of expertise, that being found in standing committees. In some legislatures, however, there are no standing committees. But even the expertise that develops in committees is diluted by the high turnover rate in many legislatures (particularly at the state level) and by legislators shifting from committee to committee. What expertise does develop in legislatures comes from longevity on the job in contrast to the specialized professional training increasingly acquired by administrators before they join the public service. In point of fact the occupational background of most legislators is the law and legal training does not prepare a person for dealing with the variety of technical problems, such as nuclear power, international finance, and cancer research, that increasingly take up the time of legislatures.

Moreover, the collegial nature of most legislatures does not suit them for making coherent attacks on problems presented to them for solution. The few centers of power are either the baronies and dukedoms held by parochial committee chairpersons jealous of their prerogatives and power or the frequently weak party leadership.

An additional liability legislatures operate under is their size. They are typically rather small in absolute numbers. The representation and expertise afforded a country of over two hundred million population by a group of 435 members of Congress or the deliberative and analytic capability of a municipal council of a dozen or so acting on behalf of a city of a quarter-million hardly seems adequate. In comparison with the personnel resources found in the executive branch, almost three million in the civilian federal service alone, the size of legislatures is indeed puny. Although legislative staffing is increasing, it still does not begin to approach the size of the executive's staffs.

Because of the increasing reliance on professionals capable of handling the many technical problems facing society, the role and power of legislatures, according to some analysts, has diminished vis-à-vis the executive branch over the last few decades. For instance, popular opinion knows that legislatures pass laws and assumes that laws originate in the legislatures. This is emphatically not the case. Most of the legislation introduced in Congress originally comes from the bureaus. Agencies, after all, are in more immediate contact with the clientele who are dissatisfied with the present form of legislation. Moreover, agency personnel themselves may be dissatisfied with existing legislation and seek its elaboration, refinement, or extension. The chief public servant, the president, in his annual state of the union message presents to Congress the legislative innovations he will send to Congress for consideration. In general legislative matters Congress is put in the position of reacting to executive initiatives.

Even when legislatures pass laws, they are often **skeletal legislation.** That is to say, the statutes spell out goals, set up general provisions, and then leave the crucial specifics to be determined by the implementing agency because the agency personnel presumably have the expertise to make the rules wisely.

The problems facing governments today often require immediate action. Certainly international crises can and do arise with frightening speed. Collegial bodies are by their very nature slow moving. Hence the initiative is almost always taken by the executive branch.

One should not get the idea that legislatures do little or nothing. It has been suggested that the press of events and the technical capability to meet problems point to the executive branch for action. Legislatures are deliberative bodies and their role has increasingly become that of ruminating on, modifying, and deciding on the desirability of what the executive branch proposed. Though the fact versus value dichotomy is too black and white to fit reality, one might suggest that it has become the role of the executive branch to present the facts of the situation and to offer alternative ways to remedy the problem. Legislators, in this interpretation, weigh the proferred alternatives in the light of values they feel should dominate or do dominate in their constituencies.

Given the general legislative role of reviewing, modifying, and analyzing proposals coming from the executive branch, it should come as no surprise that the same sequence of events should occur regarding the budget. Certainly the legislators are not conversant enough with the details of every agency's operation so that they could estimate the costs involved in present programs, let alone being able to project what it would cost for programs planned in the future. Consequently the executive branch begins the first of four phases in the budget cycle by preparing requests for an allocation of money, called the **budget-preparation phase.**

The second phase puts the ball back in the legislature's court because it then proceeds to determine the wisdom and political desirability of what is proposed by the executive branch. This **approval phase** of the budget cycle is probably the only phase that is explicitly mandated in the Constitution where it says that "No money shall be drawn from the Treasury, but in Consequence of Appropriations made by Law."

After the legislature has approved a plan for spending money in particular ways, the cycle is not complete. In the third phase of the budget cycle, the **execution or spending phase,** the initiative is once again with the executive. Legislative direction is not always sufficiently specific so as to determine exactly where and how every penny should be spent. Furthermore, circumstances change and administrators are given or manage to assume some degree of latitude in spending to meet the ever-changing exigencies of program execution.

Once money has been spent by the agencies the legislatures, and to some degree staff agencies of the executive branch, attempt to learn whether the necessary administrative latitude had been abused. In the fourth phase of the budget cycle — called the **audit or the review phase** — the legislature engages in its oversight role to determine, at the very least, whether the monies appropriated by it in the approval phase were legally expended. There is currently a trend for this oversight, carried out in the federal government by the

General Accounting Office, to move beyond questions of legality to asking whether the funds were spent efficiently and whether the funds were effective in doing what Congress intended.

Before the budget cycle is further elaborated, it must be put into perspective. Money generally cannot be appropriated for a particular agency or program until that agency or program has been authorized. Put rather simplistically, the **authorizing legislation** is like a fishing license; it allows the agency to seek funding, sometimes up to a certain limit. The appropriations process is like the fishing trip in which fish are actually caught, though not usually up to the limit. Legislation creating or authorizing, say, an Office of Saline Water and putting a limit on how much it could spend would have originated in a Natural Resources Committee in the legislature and would have been passed by the entire legislature. Legislation allowing the Office of Saline Water to spend specific amounts of money in particular years begins in the appropriations committees and then goes to the entire legislature. It is assumed in what follows that the agency is in existence and has legislation that authorizes it to spend money. Getting the money and spending it is the subject of the book.

TIMING IN THE BUDGET CYCLE

The presentation of the budget cycle so far has been in terms of motivation, logic, and a sequence of events. In the real world of budgeting the cycle is perceived in terms of specific time periods (weeks, months, years, bienniums). While there is significant variation from state to state, city to city, federal to state, state to city, and so on in the concrete time periods involved, there is substantial similarity. For the purposes of illustration, the federal cycle will be presented, followed by a discussion of how it differs from the cycle in other jurisdictions.

The notion of the **fiscal year** (abbreviated FY) is central to any understanding of the budget cycle. The fiscal year is supposed to be coterminous with the execution phase of the cycle. But the year of spending does not usually coincide with the calendar year (usually abbreviated CY) that runs from January 1 through December 31. The fiscal year for the federal government runs from October 1 of one year until September 30 of the next. There is nothing sacrosanct about the fiscal year's beginning and ending points. Up until 1976 the federal fiscal year ran from July 1 through June 30, a fiscal year that most states and many municipalities observe. Still others, however, have their starting points in other months. Since the twelve-month fiscal year does not coincide with the calendar year, a convention is used to reduce confusion. The fiscal year is usually identified by the year in which it ends. Consequently the federal fiscal year from October 1, 1977, through September 30, 1978, is referred to as Fiscal Year 1978 (frequently abbreviated to FY1978 or simply FY78). Sometimes, however, a jurisdiction will identify its fiscal year by giving both the initial and terminal year, for example, FY1977–78.

Most fiscal years are twelve months long. This is a reasonable length of time inasmuch as anything shorter would require too much preparation and approval time and effort. Anything much longer would give the executive branch too long a time to go "unsupervised" by the approval process. In the Commonwealth of Kentucky and other states, however, the fiscal year is really two years long. This is because the constitutions of those states only allow the legislatures to meet every other year. In Kentucky, in fact, the legislature is prohibited from sitting in regular sessions longer than sixty days. Because the general assembly meets only every other year, there can only be a budget approved every other year and what is approved must govern the spending of the state for a two-year period. Despite the **biennium,** as the two-year period is called, the execution phase generally is divided into two twelve-month periods for purposes of supervision. In a state with a biennial budget it is common to give both the beginning and ending years, such as FY1976–78.

Given the complications that seem to arise because the calendar and fiscal years differ, it is logical to ask why there is such a difference. One reason lies in the need for legislative approval of budgets. Most elections for public office in this country occur in the fall, usually in November, with the victors taking office after the new calendar year begins. Because the process of approving a budget can be lengthy, the newly elected legislators must be allowed enough time to evaluate and modify the budget presented to them by the executive before it must go into effect. Thus the fiscal year starts months after the calendar year begins.

The entire budget cycle, although it is based on the twelve-month execution phase, is much longer than that. To give a specific length for the entire cycle in general terms is clearly impossible as it varies from jurisdiction to jurisdiction. The timing of the phases of the federal budget cycle will be presented and some differences between that cycle and others will be brought out.

Consider fiscal year 1979 for the federal government. That year runs from

October 1, 1978, through September 30, 1979. But the budget cycle for that fiscal year began in the spring of 1977. The budget preparation phase gets under way in the spring when the president and agencies first start to plan what they will ask of Congress. The period from spring through the end of 1977 is spent in preparing, justifying, and coordinating the requests of all the spending units of the federal government. From January 1978 through September 1978 the approval phase takes place. During this time Congress examines what the executive branch plans to accomplish and finally approves some version of the request made by the executive. The execution phase of FY1979 runs from October 1978 through September 1979 and in this phase the spending units obligate and actually disburse much of the money they have been allowed. The last phase, the audit or postexecution phase, begins in October 1979 and runs on for some months. This phase, in which legislative and executive watch-dog units examine the legality, efficiency, and effectiveness of expenditures made in the execution phase, varies in length depending on the tenacity of the auditors, other demands on their time, and what they find. The total length of one budget cycle in the federal system runs, in this case, from spring 1977 probably through the beginning of 1980, almost three years.

In smaller governments the length of the cycle will usually be shorter. Obviously there is less analysis and coordination involved in preparing a municipal budget of $40 million or $4 million compared to the federal budget, which for FY1977 was about $400 billion. Similarly, less time is required to examine, modify, and approve a budget of $40 million than one of $400 billion. The same argument holds for the audit phase: The fewer the expenditures, the less there is to audit.

At the state level there is one not uncommon situation that causes a long budget cycle even though the absolute size of the budgets in those states is not very large. As mentioned earlier, a number of states operate under a biennial budget, which means that the execution phase is two years long, and this can extend the length of the total budget cycle even though the preparation, approval, and audit components are not very long.

The length of the budget cycle complicates understanding the budget process because at any one point a government can be involved in four different phases of four different fiscal years. June of 1978, for example, marks the budget preparation phase for FY1980, the approval phase of the budget for FY1979, the execution phase of the budget of FY1978, and very likely part of the audit or postexecution segment of the FY1977 budget.

The overlapping of various budget cycles does not cause any grave complications for the legislature since it is really only involved in the approval phase. The audit phases can overlap approval phases; but because the auditing is generally done by an agency working for the legislature or independent of both the legislature and the executive, the overlap causes no complication. In the executive branch, however, there is at any one time spending of money from one fiscal year, defending of requests for money for the following year, and planning of requests for the year after that. Budgeting for the agency is consequently a year-round activity. Although its cyclic nature may suggest a distinct series of stages, the length of the cycle guarantees simultaneous involvement in all phases of various cycles for the agency executive.

The complexity and sequential nature of the timing of the budget process puts a premium on meeting deadlines. Two times or changes of phase are the most crucial: the presentation of the budget requests to the legislature for review and approval of some appropriation for agency expenditure. In general the executive branch, perhaps because it has no mandated starting point, does present a document bearing all the requests for money at the appointed deadline, January in the case of the federal government. But legislatures do not always complete action of the budget requests in time for the new fiscal year. This is understandable, if not acceptable, given the composition and structure of legislatures. Congress, for example, is a body with multiple power centers located in its committees, its partisan leadership, its ideological blocs, and its state delegations, among other cleavages. In a collegial body such as this, particularly when such traditions as the filibuster exist in the Senate, there is less likelihood that deadlines will be met. Indeed, in the late 1960s and early 1970s it was not at all unusual for appropriations bills to be still unapproved and passed into law when the new fiscal year began.

If the legislative body does not pass an appropriations bill by the beginning of the new fiscal year, what happens? Money is appropriated for a precise period of time, the actual fiscal year. Money from the appropriation cannot usually be obligated for expenditure before the beginning of that period or after it ends. Should money designated for expenditure during the fiscal year not be obligated when the fiscal year ends, it usually cannot be carried over to the next fiscal year but reverts back to the treasury. In the case where the fiscal year ends and no new appropriation has been made, the agencies have no legal right to spend money. But since government operations are considered crucial and hence cannot be halted even though the legislature cannot decide on the amount to be given to the agencies, legislatures will routinely pass a **continuation appropriation** bill. Such a bill allows the agencies to spend money at the rate at which they were spending it during the just expired fiscal year until the new appropriation bill is passed. The continuation budget bill gives the legislature a breathing space and allows it to stretch the otherwise fixed timing of the budget cycle.

PHASES OF THE BUDGET PROCESS

BUDGET PREPARATION

The formulation of the budget, that is to say, the preparation of the requests that will be presented to the legislature for consideration and, it is hoped, approval, is a rather complicated process. Given the collegial and decentralized nature of legislatures, it is understandable that the approval phase may take time; but the hierarchically organized executive branch with one chief executive in charge generates the expectation of quick, straightforward, and decisive action. But contrary to popular belief, the executive branch of government is not monolithic. In reality the executive branch of almost all governmental jurisdictions is closer to a kingdom composed of many dukedoms and baronies, each professing fealty to the king, each operating so as to please the king when possible, but each guarding its own autonomy and territory against unwanted incursions from the monarch. In the budget preparation process this illustration is apt. The chief administrative officer has the last word, but he or she must gain the compliance of the subordinate agencies by either the carrot or the stick and usually by both. This interaction process can therefore be quite intricate.

Most governmental units in this country operate under an **executive budget.** This means that the chief executive officer is responsible for formulating the document composed of the requests he or she wishes the legislature to approve. Prior to the widespread adoption of the executive budget, requests for money for the coming fiscal year were generally formulated at the agency or departmental level and forwarded directly to the legislature for approval, completely bypassing the chief executive. Yet the chief executive was, at least in the popular mind, held responsible for the activities of the agencies. He or she had the responsibility without the power. By giving the chief executive power to determine what an agency requests of the legislature it was felt that corruption and mismanagement would lessen. An additional rationale for the executive budget was that, in theory at least, a president, governor, or mayor was elected because of his or her stands on issues. Controlling what the agencies seek to do by controlling what money they are allowed to ask of the legislature strengthens the linkage between what voters want as expressed in the voting booth and what voters get from the administrative agencies.

Chief executives are therefore expected to present to the legislature for approval a budget that reflects their policy priorities as well as good and efficient management. This requires the balancing of the chief executive's own policy preferences with the available resources projected to be in the treasury as well as with the policy desires of each of the agencies in the executive branch. Each agency naturally would like to see its activities funded very generously, which means getting approval from the chief executive. If every agency were allowed to get what it sought for its programs, the total request would be many times more money than would be available. The sequence of events in the preparation of the executive budget therefore can be viewed as the process of adjustment between a series of executive branch personnel.

The sequence of events in preparing an executive budget usually begins with the chief executive getting estimates from an economic and revenue staff. In the federal government the president receives relevant information from members of the Council of Economic Advisors, from the Secretary of the Treasury and staff members, and from the Director of the Office of Management and Budget. The CEA gives the president projections on the state of the economy during the fiscal year being considered. These are, it must be remembered, projections and not infallible prophecies. The tentative nature of these projections is understandable given that the economists are prognosticating conditions eighteen to thirty months in the future.

Using the information from the CEA and its own sources, the Treasury Department makes projections about the probable revenues in the upcoming fiscal year. The budget office also can make available estimates of what it would cost to fund current programs in the target fiscal year, sometimes called the current services budget. The president, using all this information, makes some broad policy decisions about the level of spending to be recommended. Political as well as programmatic factors will influence the president's initial decisions here. There may be an already established set of commitments to certain policies, such as a strong military posture, increased energy research, retrenchment of regulatory activities, or expansion of educational activities.

Similarly, political pressures and promises may dictate the presentation of a balanced budget or proposal of a large deficit to stimulate a sluggish economy. Using the information at hand and influenced by various forces, the president makes some tentative decisions about the level of spending overall and in some areas at this time. These decisions usually act as ceilings, under or at which agencies will have to prepare their requests for approval by the president.

In state and local governments the sequence of events is similar to the process just described, but with one major difference. The chief executive, be it a governor or mayor, also solicits estimates of revenue and attempts to set spending targets, overall and in specific program areas, that satisfy his or her policy preferences, political obligations, and other constraints. The only option the nonfederal governments usually lack is an ability to plan a deficit for the operating budget. Whereas the federal government can go into debt by borrowing and can plan to do this, other governments generally must propose spending no more than they expect to receive in taxes. It happens that states or cities may, in the actual execution of their budgets, not have enough revenues to cover their planned expenditures, but such a turn of events would usually be illegal if intended. Oftentimes the purchase of capital goods by governments is presented to the legislature in a **capital budget** comprised only of such expenditures. Capital budgets are often financed by bonds and so are by definition deficit spending. Discussion in this book is limited to operating budgets.

The projection of expected revenues can be a rather tricky task. Given that the revenue projection is taking place so far ahead of the actual collection of money, there is ample opportunity for error. Chief executives, particularly at the state and local levels, consequently have an incentive for making or acting on conservative revenue estimates. This conservative or economy orientation creates some tension between the higher level of the executive branch and the lower levels, where a more expansionist philosophy dominates.

Although overall spending levels are set and policy commitments are made at the highest executive levels, the budget requests made of the legislature are made on an agency-by-agency and, in some cases, on a program-by-program basis. Since the chief executive cannot prepare the budget requests at that level of detail, agencies are next called upon to make detailed requests for the resources they desire for the upcoming fiscal year. To ensure that the ceilings will be observed and some uniformity and comparability in requests will be practiced, overall guidelines for budget document preparation and submission are enforced by the central budget office.

The **central budget office** or **budget bureau** is the staff agency, usually attached to the chief executive's office, that has basic responsibility for the formulation of the budget. In its earlier forms it was basically a clerical operation that collected the requests made by the government bureaus, compiled them into one uniform format, and had copies of this document along with supporting justification material available for presentation to the legislature for review. Today the central budget office is usually a powerful policy-making agency that interprets chief executive policies to the agencies, judges the validity and acceptability of agency requests, and makes almost final decisions about what an agency can request of the legislature.

After the general policies are set by the chief executive the budget bureau usually sends out to all spending units detailed instructions for the submission of requests. These instructions can be procedural, substantive, or both. Document 1 in the documents appendix, for example, is a reproduction of instructions from the budget office in the Commonwealth of Kentucky that gives specific substantive instructions about how much money can be requested for various objects of expenditure. The figures for postage, heating, and the like implement overall ceilings and policy positions taken by the governor.

Instructions oriented to more procedural matters are seen in document 2. These instructions on how to fill out various forms used in the federal government's budget submission process illustrate the need for standardized information in the Office of Management and Budget. The information acquired through the forms sent to the budget office assists the budget office in determining which requests are truly justified, which are marginal, and which are unsupportable.

So far in the sequence of events leading to the final budget requests the chief executive has made some overall policy decisions that are sent to the spending units, which begin to prepare what they want in accordance with guidelines set out by the central budget office. While the executive branch of government is not monolithic, it is hierarchically arranged and anything proposed at the lower levels must be approved at intermediate and upper levels. So, too, with budget preparation. For purposes of coherence most agencies are located together with allied or related agencies in departments. The departmental leadership has the responsibility for seeing, among other things, that agencies do not act at cross purposes and for setting priorities among the programs being implemented or being proposed by the agencies under them.

Consequently, all agencies must next get their budget requests approved by department-level officials. Departmental personnel examine the requests made by the agencies, analyze the justifications for the proposals, and modify the requests to keep within spending limits set for the department. Personnel at this level also attempt to set their own priorities by allowing requests for some programs while modifying or denying requests for others. In some jurisdictions there are actual hearings held at this level in which agency personnel argue for their budget requests before departmental policy and budget personnel.

After the department has approved the requests from agencies, those requests must then be reviewed by the central budget office to guarantee conformity with the policy priorities and the spending ceilings set by the chief executive. Just as at the departmental level, in some governments there are hearings before officials of the central budget office. These hearings serve at least two purposes. For one the budget office can judge the merit of the proposals and attempt to weld all the various requests into a coherent package. But for the agency personnel these hearings can serve as practice or a dry run for the hearings they will take part in before the legislature.

In general the decisions of the central budget office are final. Budget personnel are well aware of the desires of the chief executive and attempt to implement them. Obviously there are misinterpretations from time to time as well as agency and departmental-level personnel who are not willing to accept a budget officer's decision as final. In these cases an appeal is made to the chief executive for a final decision. At this point, in the federal government approximately six to eight months after the preparation phase began, there may have been changes in the revenue forecast, the political situation, or the policy preferences of the chief executive. At the last moment there may, consequently, be final adjustments and modifications of the requests made to the legislature.

The very last steps in the preparation phase of the budget cycle are the printing of the document that includes the requests of all spending units for the next fiscal year and the delivery of this document to the legislature by the chief executive, usually with a speech setting out the highlights of the budget proposals.

BUDGET APPROVAL

This phase of the process begins with an executive initiative in the form of the budget document itself and ends with the passage of a law allowing agencies to obligate specified amounts of money. In some regards this phase of the process is the same as the passage of any bill into law, but there are a few differences. No appropriations bill ever dies in committee. Most appropriations bills are handled very expeditiously. Most bills involve the same legislators, the same agency personnel, and the same interest group participants. And most appropriations bills review substantially the same material from year to year.

In most governments it is appropriate to speak of the appropriations bill inasmuch as the amounts of money for all spending units are incorporated into one bill. However in some jurisdictions there are many bills. In the federal government, for example, there usually are twelve or thirteen separate bills, each covering the funding of one portion of the government's activity. Consequently, there is one bill for the departments of Labor and Health, Education and Welfare, another for State, Commerce, and Treasury, and still another for Interior and related agencies.

Whatever the number of appropriations bills, the approval process begins with the budget document being transmitted to the legislature, where it is sent to the committee or committees responsible for appropriations. Document 3 in the appendix is a typical page of a federal budget document. The columns marked "estimate" contain the requested funding.

The document composed of all the budget requests is not the sole basis upon which the committee decision is made. The committee also holds hearings on the agency requests wherein each agency's top administrators appear and personally defend what they desire. To bolster their case, justification material in addition to what the budget document contains is provided to the committee by each agency. This usually describes in great detail how much is proposed for each program or activity or object in the request for the new fiscal year. Additionally, the justification materials describe what activities have been carried out in the past in an attempt to convince the committee of the value of the agency's operation. To generate further information, interest group representatives, interested private citizens, and interested legislators also testify before the committees.

The appropriations committee, after it hears all the testimony, generally goes into executive session and discusses the merits of the budget requests and the testimony on those requests. After those deliberations a decision is made and the committee issues a report of its deliberations, containing the level of funding it deems proper and the reasons for its recommendations.

Document 4 in the appendix reproduces two pages from a Senate Appropriations Committee report.

Next the entire chamber receives the appropriations committee report, which is usually unanimous. This reports on the appropriations bill that has been introduced by a legislator incorporating the appropriations committee's recommendations on the requests made by the chief executive. Document 5 in the appendix is a portion of the bill for the appropriations for the federal departments of Labor and Health, Education and Welfare. Note that this bill is not in the same format as the report or the budget document. It is essentially a summary of the money allowed to the agency and it, when passed into law, is the only legally binding constraint on the agency. However, all the discussion and comments at the hearing as well as desires expressed in the report will be seriously considered by a prudent administrator.

Following debate on the floor of the legislature, the bill as amended is generally passed and sent to the chief executive for signing into law or, if a bicameral legislature is involved, sent to the other chamber for consideration. In the other chamber the process just described recurs. The bill is sent to committee for consideration. Hearings are scheduled, testimony is heard, decisions are made, a report is issued, the bill is debated, and a vote is taken. If the bill passed in the second chamber is the same as the bill passed in the first, the appropriations bill is sent to the chief executive for signature. If not, a conference committee is appointed of members from both houses, usually members from the appropriations committees of both houses, to sort out the differences between the two versions. When some agreement is reached, the compromise version of the bill goes to each chamber, where it is accepted in toto or rejected. Assuming acceptance, the bill then goes to the chief executive for signature into law.

Although the process just outlined describes most governments' budget approval processes, there is obviously variation from jurisdiction to jurisdiction. In larger governments having multiple appropriations bills, subcommittees of the appropriations committee do most of the work by holding the hearings and issuing the reports. Smaller governments generally can complete this phase in much shorter time than larger governments, and from one jurisdiction to the next there is great variety in the depth and shrewdness with which legislators analyze and scrutinize executive agency requests.

It should be noted that in most governments the budget approval process is largely reactive and fragmented. It is reactive in the sense that the legislature responds to budget requests made by the executive branch. It is fragmented because there is usually little coordination between the spending or appropriations committees and the funding or revenue committees. It is even more fragmented where appropriations subcommittees in effect pass parts or whole appropriations bills without coordination with the other subcommittees. This fragmentation and reaction behavior has caused legislatures to be criticized for irresponsibility. One reform that attempts to coordinate and rationalize the budget approval phase was recently initiated in the U.S. Congress with passage of the Budget Control and Impoundment Act of 1974.[2] To demonstrate how legislatures can increase their responsiveness and enhance the coherence of their policies as well as to illustrate how the budget approval process can become very complicated, some highlights of the new federal budget approval process are presented.

In both houses of Congress the committees in charge of government spending are the appropriations committees; those responsible for raising money are the House Ways and Means Committee and the Senate Finance Committee. Until recently each went its own way. This could and did occasionally put the country more in the red than the president had advocated. Moreover, no attempt was made to set overall congressional policy priorities through the budget. These defects were remedied to some degree by the creation of a Senate Budget Committee and a House Budget Committee and by the institution of a few new procedures in the budget approval process.

The role of budget committees is to propose resolutions setting overall spending ceilings and spending ceilings in particular policy areas such as national defense, health, agriculture, and so on. They do this with the technical assistance of the Congressional Budget Office, a newly created congressional staff body somewhat analogous to the president's Office of Management and Budget. The CBO makes estimates of the economic situation and revenues likely in the fiscal year under consideration. The budget committees introduce a resolution that is scheduled for passage by May 15 of every year that sets the ceilings referred to earlier. The passage of this resolution involves members of Congress from appropriations, revenue, and substantive policy area committees and so is likely to assist in compliance with the ceilings. The appropriations committees proceed as they would normally, taking testimony and deciding how much to recommend for each agency but keeping in mind the spending ceilings now binding them. By September 15 a second budget resolution is introduced that may modify the one passed in May because of changes in circumstances. This resolution can reconcile appropriations committee and congressional decisions on spending with projected revenues by either cutting spending or raising taxes to meet the limits to which Congress has agreed. This reform is meant to add a certain degree of coherence to policy formulation and implementation in Congress as well as rescuing this body from charges of fiscal irresponsibility.

BUDGET EXECUTION

Once the fiscal year has begun and the appropriations bill has passed, the agencies have what amounts to a bank account. They are allowed to spend the dollar amount listed in the appropriations act. It should be noted that the passage of an appropriations bill really gives the agency **obligational authority** or **new obligational authority.** This means that in the fiscal year funded the agency need not actually expend the money but need only contract to spend money, to obligate the treasury. The actual **outlay** of money from the treasury may be in the next fiscal year, and money spent in this year may have been appropriated in previous fiscal years. The distinction between budget obligations and budget outlays can cause complications in assessing the impact of government spending inasmuch as the timing of the actual disbursement of money may not be easily under the control of the administration executing a budget.

Although most appropriations acts merely mention a dollar figure with no qualifications, there are many constraints binding how, when, and for what "their" money can be spent. Certainly administrative agencies require a fair degree of latitude in their operation. Agencies with thousands of employees and thousands of clients need some freedom of action. But that latitude can be and has been abused in the past. Keeping in mind that agencies generally do not get all the money they desire from the department, the central budget office, or the legislature, there is a tendency to spend money faster than they should. In fact, in the past it was not unknown for an agency to spend the money appropriated to it for a twelve-month period in less than a year. Since agencies at least theoretically provide needed services, it simply would not do to close up shop for two or three months until new money is made available. The chief executive was therefore forced to ask the legislature for money to tide the agency over until the next fiscal year. While there are legitimate reasons for such **supplemental appropriations,** administrative prodigality is not one of them. To prevent such improvident spending, all money appropriated to an agency is apportioned or allotted to the agency by the central budget office.

As an example of **apportionment,** assume an agency is appropriated $12 million. The central budget office may dole out the money to the agency or, to be more accurate, may allow the agency to obligate the money for specific purposes on a $1-million-per-month or a $3-million-a-quarter basis. Allotment may also be by major categories of expenditures. Similarly, the central budget office through the same mechanism can reserve, say 5 percent of all appropriations to prepare for unforeseeable events. If an agency's workload is not steady but varies seasonally, the apportionment process will usually reflect that. Thus, a bureau of parks whose activities are heaviest in the summer months would have more of its money available for spending in the summer than in the winter.

Similar to apportionment, the chief executive office in some jurisdictions can impound funds. This means that the chief executive views the appropriation act as permissive and not mandatory. **Impoundment** means that on an item-by-item or program-by-program basis the chief executive simply refuses to let the agency spend money. Although this may hinder agency-level discretion, it still is an indication of executive branch initiative vis-à-vis the legislature. When impoundment is used to nullify legislative intent, conflict beween the branches of government arises. While Congress allowed and even encouraged impoundment by the president since the early days of the Republic, brash and impudent impoundment by President Nixon caused Congress to apply strict conditions to the practice of impoundment as seen in provisions of the 1974 budget reform legislation. Under the provisions of that legislation the president can defer spending money appropriated by Congress unless either chamber passes a resolution disallowing the **deferral.** To not obligate the money appropriated, called a **recission,** the president must get both houses of Congress to pass a resolution that agrees with the president's proposed recission, which is not a simple task.

Although formal, legal legislative control over executive branch spending is found only in the appropriations act itself, agency personnel know that the detail about the purposes, the activities, and the programs spelled out in the budget document and the justification materials presented to the legislature are to be viewed as promises about how the appropriated money will be spent. Moreover, the line of questioning in the hearings and the admonitions and recommendations in committee reports give information regarding how the legislature wants the money spent. All of this is best heeded, even though it is not always heeded.

Agency personnel take the initiative in spending away from the legislature at times through the practice of **reprogramming.**[3] The legislature, for instance, allocated money for program A but not for the proposed program B. The driving need for program A never materializes while B becomes more attractive. The agency therefore shifts money to implement program B. The Defense Department has proven particularly adept at this type of maneuver. Eventually the legislature finds out about the shift of money from one purpose to another, but not until the change has been made.

To prevent wholesale changing of legislatively approved priorities by agencies under the banner of administrative latitude, legislatures sometimes set a dollar figure under which agencies can move money around but over which approval must be secured from appropriation committee personnel prior to reprogramming.

Yet another way in which agency executives can spend money without formal appropriations committee approval is through **backdoor spending.** Agencies can sometimes legally spend money by going outside the appropriations route through **contract and loan authority.** A substantive committee may get legislation passed that authorizes an agency to enter into contracts that will require the subsequent expenditure of money. Since the agency legally obligated the government to spend money in the future, when that time comes the appropriations committee and the rest of the legislature are forced to give the money. Similarly, some agencies have the authority to make loans. When they do so, the treasury must honor the loan commitment and the money must be made available. In these and in similar cases monies are expended through the back door, that is, outside the regular appropriations process and consequently outside the control of committees theoretically in control of spending. Executive initiative here forces legislative compliance.

Backdoor spending can be controlled by funneling all expenditures through a central legislative body or a required procedure. The federal budget reform legislation attempts to do this by making almost all expenditures, back door or front door, subject to the overall and functional ceilings.

POSTEXECUTION OR AUDIT PHASE

Recognizing that the approval of money for expenditure does not guarantee that the money is spent properly, legislatures often wait until the fiscal year is over and then send in people to examine how money was spent. For instance, at the federal level the General Accounting Office regularly checks to see if agencies properly spent their money. There are, at the state level, auditing agencies that are independent of both the legislature and the executive. And within the executive branch auditing personnel operate to guarantee legality. All of these institutions are engaged in closing the barn door after the horse has fled. Guilty parties are identified and prosecuted as a result of such activity, but the most important contribution of this activity is in identifying what went wrong.

Many years ago the prime concern in the postexecution phase was the legality of agency expenditures. Today legislators are more interested in how agencies operate. Perhaps because the incidence of corruption in government has dropped and perhaps because of a greater interest in controlling the efficiency and effectiveness of executive action, audit units are moving into performance and effectiveness analysis. Since the sequence of events and timing in these activities does not condition other actions in the cycle, no more will be said about the postexecution phase.

This chapter has presented the budget process conceptually and then sequentially. The explanation has been descriptive of who does what and when. The results of the interaction have not been covered and the motivations and characteristics of the actors have not been behaviorally analyzed. Those concerns are dealt with in the next chapter.

SUMMARY

Periodic approval of money about to be spent by the executive branch of government aids in making government responsive to the people. The process by which money is appropriated is referred to as the budget cycle. In the first or formulation stage the executive branch personnel prepare requests for money that they feel is needed to carry out their programs. In the second or approval phase executive branch requests are presented to the legislators, who evaluate, modify, and finally pass an appropriation bill that embodies their wishes and, theoretically, the desires of their constituents. In the third or execution phase the money appropriated by the legislature is spent, or, more properly, obligated for expenditure. Lastly, in the audit or postexecution phase the legislature through a bureaucratic arm examines whether the executive branch spent the money given it according to the letter of the appropriations law passed by the legislature.

The sequence of events just outlined is the same in every government juris-diction although the length of the stages and the starting and end points of the cycle may vary. The sequence of events with alternation from the executive initiative to legislative approval, through executive implementation, and ending with legislative checking up on executive action serves to prevent spending of tax money without due control by elected officials.

NOTES

1. Robert D. Lee, Jr. and Ronald W. Johnson offer a similar set of questions in introduc-ing their treatment of budgeting in *Public Budgeting Systems* (Baltimore: University Park Press, 1973), pp. 4–13.

2. A description of the provisions of the new legislation and its implementation the first time is found in Joel Havemann, *The Federal Budget: Reform's First Round* (Washington, D.C.: National Journal Reprints, n.d.).

3. The process of executive budget implementation at the federal level finds excellent treatment in Lewis Fisher, *Presidential Spending Power* (Princeton, N.J.: Princeton Uni-versity Press, 1975).

SELECTED BIBLIOGRAPHY

Because of the variety in the details of any government's budget chronology, no one source can be completely authoritative. The first entry is perhaps the closest to the ideal of comprehensiveness for state governments. The remaining two entries give a reasonable presentation of the situation at the federal level. For information on local level governments the best source would be the individ-ual jurisdictions.

Bowhay, James H., and Thrall, Virginia D. *State Legislative Appropriations Process.* Lexington, Kentucky: Council of State Governments, 1975.

Havemann, Joel. *The Federal Budget: Reform's First Round.* Washington, D.C.: National Journal Reprints, n.d.

U.S., Executive Office of the President, Office of Management and Budget. *The Budget of the United States Government Fiscal Year 1976.* Washington, D.C.: Government Printing Office, 1975, pp. 162–167.

Chapter IV

BUDGETS AS GAMES:

ACTORS,

   ROLES,

AND OUTCOMES

The behavior of the market in allocating a society's resources is, at least in theory, rather lawlike. That is to say, the allocation is reasonably predictable. One can, if enough information is available, make fairly close estimates of the quantity of a good produced as well as the price at which the good will be sold. But when allocation is through a command system (by a budget process), the results are not as lawlike. To be sure, there are regular patterns of behavior and of decision making, but their predictability is less than what one expects in dealing with market allocation systems.

When politics is the engine that distributes resources through the budget process, equations such as those associated with supply and demand are not useful for understanding the allocation process. In fact, equations in general are not very useful in budgeting — so far. The behavior in politics is not so deterministic as to be susceptible to formulation in equation form. The notion of a game, however, has utility in generating an understanding of budgeting. In games most behavior is contingent upon many factors and forces that are not easily predictable. Obviously, there are regularities and patterns over the long run; but in the immediate situation guesswork, probability, intention, and a feel for the game are crucial. The same holds true in politics in general and in budgeting in particular.

To underscore this perspective on budgeting, consider the game of chess. No one can predict ahead of time which of two equally skilled players will win. But in the course of the match a judgment can be made of the techniques used, the strategies employed, and the style characterizing each player. This information can help in estimating how the match will develop. At the level of the pieces in a game of chess, further points should be made. Each piece can move in a specified manner, but that manner varies from knight to rook to bishop to queen and so on. One can predict that on a board with a rook and a pawn, the rook should always take the pawn. But it is not as clear what the outcome of a duel between a bishop and a rook would be. Further complicate the playing field with other pieces deployed to constrain the movement of the rook and bishop and the result is still less predictable.

Whatever the uncertainties in predicting who wins or who loses a chess match, understanding who the antagonists are, what pieces they have, the capabilities of the pieces, the tactics frequently used, and the philosophies of the players does allow an observer to understand the game and, in certain circumstances, make an accurate assessment of what is likely to occur.

In this chapter budgeting is presented as a game by considering the budget process as a series of interactions among various participants, each of whom has goals, resources, orientations, background, and stakes that differ from those of the other participants. Because of the variation in the resources, orientations, stakes, and so on of each actor, the end result is not preordained, even though certain patterns may emerge. The last chapter in effect spelled out the rules of the game by rather formally detailing the sequence of events. This chapter describes the characteristics of the actors and delineates some of the general patterns that have emerged in the past. Knowing the characteristics of the actors, the nature of their interaction, and the likely outcome of the interactions should assist in making the budgetary process a bit more understandable and perhaps even a little more predictable.

THE BUDGET GAME

While passing a budget can be viewed as the entire game, there are really two distinct subgames that comprise the complete game. The first scrimmage, as it were, consists of the process involved in preparing a budget document embodying the requests of the executive branch. The second subgame is the process of getting approval for the requests or some variant of the requests. The first subgame takes place primarily within the executive branch; the second centers on interaction between the legislature and the executive as well as interaction among groups in the legislative branch. The treatment that follows is therefore in two parts.

Each set of actors has been briefly introduced in the last chapter. Here they are more exhaustively covered so their behavior will be understandable, if not generally predictable. This is done by comparing them on three broad dimensions: reference and support groups, fiscal versus programmatic orientation, and professional versus political background. A word or two explaining and justifying each of these dimensions is in order.

Since the very size of our society prohibits the practice of direct democratic government, representation constantly takes place. It is well known that legislators represent those in their constituencies. But all governmental actors, legislative or executive, have constituents, people who support them. It is clear that the nature of supporters or constituents can have an important influence on what is done and how it is done. If supporters are powerful, well placed, and numerous, action can be direct and will likely be successful. Weak and diffuse support lends itself to more subtle techniques with less assurance of success.

The fiscal versus programmatic orientation basically reflects the split between spenders and savers. Some actors in the budget process are intent on providing services and goods, others focus on spending little, and still others try to strike a balance between the two more extreme orientations. The attitude one takes to spending will have an impact on the style, the justification posture, and rhetoric employed. It should also be somewhat related to the supporters one has.

Because government is involved in providing a wide variety of services, there is a great degree of specialization of labor. Increasingly this specialization of labor appears under the guise of professionalism. This means that employees become expert in dealing with some specific problem or group of clientele. This expertise leads to parochialism and narrowness of focus in the budget process for some of the actors. The narrow focus characterizing certain budget process participants can generate severe problems given the multiplicity of experts in government. Consequently, people of a broader perspective, integrators, as it were, try to pull the specializations together or to discriminate among them. This integrating or selecting is performed by making reference to nonprofessional criteria, to values that are putatively found in the populace. The people who try to judge, to select, and to take a broader perspective are usually the politicians. The difference between these two perspectives and even backgrounds will translate into use of differing kinds of arguments and into differences in the tenacity with which positions are held.

THE BUDGET PREPARATION GAME: ACTORS AND ROLES

Practically all governmental units in this country use an executive budget. That is to say the chief executive is responsible for preparing a coherent set of requests for money to run the executive branch and for presenting that set of requests to the legislature for approval. Popular conceptions notwithstanding, the executive branch of any government is not monolithic, with all parts agreeing on what should be done. There are usually five kinds of executive branch budget participants, each of which wants something different in the budget. These five actors are the agencies, the chief executive, the departments, the revenue raisers/forecasters, and the central budget office. Each of these is now discussed to make their behavior more understandable.

AGENCIES

Probably the most basic group of those involved in preparing the budget is the agency. Since agencies are the basic spending units, they are closest to the nitty-gritty of budget preparation. They are the ones that have the detailed knowledge to cost out programs and to make at least initial budget requests. What characterizes their role in budgeting? Consider first their reference or support groups.

The basic source of support for any agency is its clientele. They receive some good or service from the agency, usually at little or no direct cost, and hence are usually the mainstay of an agency's existence. For example, the relations between an employment service and the unemployed, between the Pentagon and weapons producers, between the Bureau of Reclamation and farmers in western states, between the National Science Foundation and research universities, between the Social Security Administration and the elderly, and between the Federal Communications Commission and the broadcast industry all illustrate the special relations between an agency and the public with which it is intimately connected. From these illustrations it becomes clear that some clients are more supportive of agency activity than others. Certainly the weapons producers will intensely support the Defense Department's aspirations for larger budgets because they will very directly benefit from a large defense budget. On the other hand it is unlikely that the broadcast media will unequivocally argue for higher FCC budgets because increased funds could possibly be used to regulate the activity of broadcasters.

An additional aspect of the support an agency enjoys for its activities and its budget is the power of its clientele. The unemployed would undoubtedly be pleased to see placement programs expanded, and the elderly would like expanded services provided them through Social Security, but both the unemployed and elderly lack credible power, even though they are quite numerous. Farmers and weapons producers, while few in absolute numbers, are much more influential in the country and their support for irrigation or for the military will both embolden "their" agencies to seek funding and assist them in gaining funds.

Because agencies serve outside clients, they also gain the support of certain segments of the legislature. Committees in a legislature serve specific clients.

An education committee typically has close bonds to educational institutions and instructional personnel; a banking committee usually works hand in hand with financial interests; and an agriculture committee generally has tight ties with farmers and farm organizations. When an agency serves a client group, the substantive legislative committee is pleased, because "my friend's friend is my friend."

The orientation of agencies in budget preparation is heavily programmatic and very rarely fiscal.[1] Agencies prosper — and their personnel prosper — when clients are pleased, and clients are pleased when favorable programs are operational or forthcoming. Since agency personnel do not have any responsibility for collecting money, they do not worry about balanced budgets or fiscal probity but leave such worries to others. Agencies, however, are in constant contact with substantive problems needing solutions and clients desiring service. These pressures are most immediate to agencies, far more proximate than questions of balanced budgets and revenue projection. In short, it is not the job of the agency to worry about fiscal questions; it is its job to be concerned about programs.

At the more individual level, agency personnel see their careers progress when they do their job well. To perform a function, however, requires resources. Consequently, self-interested government employees, interested only in furthering their careers, operate rationally when they try to expand agency programs because such expansion produces services for which they can take credit. If the government employee is not selfishly oriented but more altruistically driven, once again that bureaucrat would seek enhancement or expansion of agency programs. In the arena of personal incentives the agency personnel benefit when they are concerned with apprehending drug traffickers, launching missiles, processing patents, and carrying out the many programs comprising the whole of government activity rather than niggling over pennies or millions of dollars.

As one might expect, the background of government agency personnel is more professional than political. Mosher argues cogently that a major trend in the composition of the executive branch is the increasing professionalization of its members. As early as 1960 over one-third of all professionals in the country were employed by government.[2] Given that fewer than one-third of all those employed were in government service, professionals are overrepresented in the executive branch of government. Professionals are socialized through long training into norms of service toward specific groups such as the sick, the poor, or the ignorant and/or they are schooled in performing certain tasks according to standards rather rigidly specified by their peers (for example, CPAs, engineers, and economists). This professional cast of the bureaucracy signals that in budgetary matters they will try to take their cues from their relatively narrowly focused training or their particular target population.

When one puts together the narrow and professional background, the programmatic orientation, and the specific and rather clearly defined support groups, it is clear that the role or the stance of agencies in preparing their budget requests will be expansionary and probably rather aggressive. This complex of factors characterizing the agency is in conflict with the configuration of factors characterizing other actors.

CHIEF EXECUTIVES

The role configuration of the chief executive is virtually the direct opposite of the agencies: First, the reference or support group is really a series of reference and support groups. The president, governor, or mayor is usually the only person in his or her jurisdictions that is expected to represent all of the people and who is elected in a jurisdictionwide election. In point of fact, persons elected chief executive achieve that position precisely because they are able to marshal a larger, more extensive, more encompassing coalition of supporting groups than any other candidate. Numerically, by virtue of being the chief executive, that person usually has the backing of more than half of all those interested enough in the outcome of an election to cast a ballot.

Because the chief executive was elected by a collection of people who, given the heterogeneous composition of practically any governmental jurisdiction today, represent differing interests, those people must be satisfied once the candidate takes office. Getting elected means that the chief executive was able to propose a set of programs that pleased most voters or was able to talk around the issues and sell his or her image, personality, or party to the electorate. In the first case the chief executive will have priorities and policy preferences that will favor some agencies' programs and will necessarily treat other agencies' programs less well. In the situation where the executive was elected on the basis of party or personality there may not be preexisting favorites among agencies and their programs when executive office is assumed. But once in office, the chief executive is almost immediately faced with many specific and diverse demands from supporters and the realization that resources are not abundant enough to satisfy all of the demands.

The chief elected administrative official must face up to the problem of satisfying many different constituencies to fulfill campaign promises, real or implied, or to ensure reelection. To become a narrow partisan of a particular program almost certainly will alienate some supporters. To try to give a little to every program and agency will not satisfy constituents because insufficient resources guarantee that each program or agency will receive only a drop in the bucket. What solution is there to this problem? Just as in getting elected, the only solution is to put together a coalition of those supporters who can help you the most and to ignore those who can hurt you the least. Therefore chief executives will attempt to favor financially those agencies and programs that will please as many electoral supporters as possible and will slight those that have the least power to punish them or their party in the next election. Chief executives are also their own constituency. Strongly held policy preferences must also be balanced against the policy preferences of other constituents.

Whereas the orientation of the agency was overwhelmingly programmatic, the chief executive must assume both a programmatic and a fiscal posture. Support for specific programs is the means whereby supporters are rewarded. If labor unions helped a candidate get elected, worker safety and workman's compensation programs must be well funded. But the executive must also keep an eye on the treasury. To support too many programs at too high a level of funding usually means that taxes must be raised, an expedient that is sure to lose supporters at the next election. Hence a fiscal stance is also required for the chief executive.

At the federal level the fiscal orientation is not as binding as it is at the state and local levels. The president can propose an unbalanced budget. That is to say, the president can propose spending more money in the upcoming fiscal year than is expected to come into the government coffers. To make up the deficit, the government merely borrows the shortfall. Since government's credit is good, there usually is no problem in raising funds this way.

In state and local governments the chief executive must take a rather strong fiscal orientation — for two reasons. First, it is generally against the law to propose to spend more money for operating governmental programs than is expected in revenues. Consequently, governors and mayors must present balanced budgets to their legislative oversight bodies. This means that in dealing with agencies and their desires for expansion there is bound to be some conflict. Second, even in the special circumstances when borrowing is legal, not all state and local governments are equally good credit risks. When forecasts of revenue are low and financial obligations are fixed or when capital investments are financed by issuing bonds, not all jurisdictions can be counted on to manage their money wisely and lending institutions will be wary of extending credit.

With regard to the background of the chief executive it is safe to say that political rather than professional is the best characterization. Since chief executive officers are elected, and usually elected in partisan contests, their skills and background are in the integrator or facilitator class. They are not committed to the narrow concerns of professionals, to very specific problems, or to a particular substantive skill but rather seek to paper over differences and to seek consensus and commonality.

If there is any one training that forms the background of most politicians in general, and even chief executives in particular, it is legal training. Passage of the bar and the practice of law admirably suits involvement in politics. For one, involvement with statutes and their writing gives an edge to an attorney. Second, the practice of law can be left to partners while a lawyer runs for and holds office. Third, should one leave office, the contacts made in political life can enhance the law firm's business. Even while in office one can make contacts that will assist the firm. Many other factors also make the study and practice of law a congenial background for political life. But one final point should be made about legal training and the practice of law. Attorneys are essentially advocates. That is to say, their skills are desired by those in conflict with other parties. The skills of the attorney are directed to maximizing the benefit of the client, but this is very frequently done by compromise. For every case that goes to court, many conflicts are resolved by compromise and bargaining between legal counsel. These skills in resolving conflict while seeking optimal benefits for one's backers obviously serve a person well in politics.

In the budget process, then, the chief executive can be expected to put together compromises while trying to retain supporters by selectively supporting certain programs. Because of campaign promises specific agencies may be favored relative to others, but because of revenue limitations few agencies are likely to get as much as they wish from the chief executive.

The agencies and the chief executive represent the polar extremes of those involved in preparing the executive budget. In between are participants who, in effect, bring into concert those polar positions or, in some cases at least, act to bring the agencies into line with the chief executive's wishes. The two major actors in this effort are those in the central budget office and the department-level executives. But before those budget participants are examined, it is important to consider some relatively minor actors. These set the stage for both the chief executive and the agencies and all those in between.

REVENUE RAISERS/FORECASTERS

Because of legal constraints that frequently require a balanced budget and because of popular opinion that desires a balanced budget, before chief executives can make even general programmatic commitments they must have some notion of what revenue can be expected in the fiscal year under consideration. Since presidents, governors, and mayors are not skilled or qualified to make such estimates, they turn to the personnel of the treasury or tax collecting bureaus and, in larger governmental units, to government economists.

Government income is derived from many sources: taxes on personal income, on corporate income, on property, on sales, on use, on transactions, on imports, and on exports, to name but a few of the major ones. Even if the rates of taxation are fixed, it still is no easy matter to estimate income. The economy is always in some state of flux with, say, personal income rising and falling or rising at different rates in differents parts of the workforce. Estimating income requires a comprehensive knowledge of the sources of income and the rates of taxation, knowledge that usually is found in the Treasury Department. In addition to that, forecasting requires competence in projecting the state of the economy through the fiscal year whose budget is being prepared. It is of little value to know that the current tax rates will bring in X million dollars in revenue if next year is like this year when there is every likelihood that next year will be less prosperous. Here the economists come into play by attempting to project the kind of economy likely to occur. This knowledge, along with knowing the tax rates, should allow an accurate estimate of income.

Revenue estimators can assist the chief executive in another way. If certain expenditures must be made and if the projected income will not cover the required expenditures, it is necessary to change tax rates or to impose new taxes. Treasury officials and economists are usually the source of proposals for such technical changes. They usually attempt to suggest tax rates and tax sources that will be equitable and dependable. Where the budget does not have to be balanced, as at the federal level, readjustment of tax rates does not have to be part of the budget process. At more local levels the chief executive budget proposals are more frequently tied in with tax changes.

In larger governmental jurisdictions revenue forecasting is more likely to be done by a specialized unit.[3] The federal government uses the Council of

Economic Advisors, a group of highly regarded professional economists, to project the state of the economy. They, and their counterparts at the state level, tend to view budgets not so much as documents giving guidelines for funding specific substantive programs, but rather as instruments through which the government can influence the state of the economy. Depending on their outlook, philosophy, and perhaps training, economic advisors may, for example, press the chief executive for deficit spending to reduce unemployment in the workforce or they may advocate a balanced budget to reduce inflation. Their philosophy as economists can have an influence on the chief executive's budget apart from the role of economic forecaster.

To further clarify the activity and the place of the revenue forecaster and economist in the budget preparation game, I now elaborate their support groups, their orientation, and their background. There are two basic support and reference groups for revenue personnel: the chief executive and their professional peers, of which the chief executive is clearly the most important. The chief executive's entire budget proposal is based on the amount of money projected to be available and perhaps on the deficit size counseled by the forecasters and economists. If the revenue projections are off the mark or if the deficit, for instance, does not bolster a sagging economy as predicted, it is the chief executive who is blamed. But in such cases the forecasters and economists find that their advice is no longer received with much favor. To retain their positions they must be accurate in giving advice. Given their backgrounds, serving one major master does not require contortions. Most people in these positions are highly trained professionals, usually with a fair amount of experience. Their training in high-level economics, taxation, and related areas imbues them with professional standards of performance. Since they are asked to do what their training prepares them for and since they are rewarded by their supporter and superior, the chief executive, for doing this well, their role in the budget process is straightforward. Because they do not generally get into specific expenditure programs, these people have very little to do with the other participants in budget preparation.

Thus the overall role of revenue forecasters and economists in this game is a rather narrow one. Most of their involvement occurs at the very beginning of the budget formulation process. They respond to one person and that person calls on them to perform tasks that are largely technical and for which they usually have been well trained. But just because their role is narrow does not mean it is unimportant. The advice given and the forecasts made set the stage for practically all that will follow. Their best estimates, in fact, constrain the behavior of the preeminent actor in the process, the chief executive.

DEPARTMENTS

It was suggested earlier that there must be accommodation between the goals and perspectives of the chief executive and those of the agencies. In most jurisdictions agencies are grouped together with similar agencies into larger administrative units called departments. For example, the Bureau of Labor Statistics, the Wage and Hour Division, the Bureau of Labor Standards, the Bureau of Apprenticeship and Training, along with other agencies comprise the federal Department of Labor. All of those agencies in some way attempt to foster the well-being of the worker; it therefore makes sense to group them together and put them under a central administrative officer, in this case the secretary of labor. It is the secretary and his or her budget staff that attempt to reconcile the pressures for programmatic enhancement from the agencies with the programmatic and fiscal guidelines set by the chief executive officer.

The job of the department-level personnel in preparing a budget is a conflicting one. Consider first the matter of support groups. Secretaries are usually chosen because they are knowledgeable in the area of the department's activity and because they will be loyal to the chief executive who appoints them. These two selection criteria can pull in opposing directions. Departmental personnel have ties to their clientele, which means that they will seek program enhancement to serve, for example, the labor movement. But at the same time they are supposed to be responsive to the chief executive officer, who may not view their programs as having a high priority. Even a chief executive who favors their programs is under certain revenue constraints that reduce the funding of favored programs. When the budget ceilings for a particular department are made known, the departmental personnel must enforce these limits on their agencies. The departments thus appear schizoid by virtue of being programmatic when dealing with the chief executive officer but fiscally oriented in dealing with their agencies.

Obviously departments are not uniformly fiscal in relations with their agencies and programmatic in arguing for programs to the chief executive. Under the guise of fiscal stringency an unwanted or inefficient program or agency can be reduced or eliminated. And programmatic concerns can be acknowledged and supported to the chief executive, but in general the two basic support or clientele groups that a department must serve require some bifurcation in orientation.

Similarly, the background of departmental personnel fits in with this dual orientation. The very top-level officials in any department are political appointees. Their role is that of the politician anywhere: practicing the art of the possible. Hence, they will recognize the need to adapt to the divergent support groups and will act to reconcile antagonistic factions. But below the level of secretary, assistant secretary, deputy secretary, undersecretary, and their assistants, the permanent civil servant takes over. The career government employee adopts much more of the professional or the advocate role. Job security allows this. While the political appointee usually stays on the job at the sufferance of the higher appointing power, the civil servant has job tenure that allows firmer stands on some issues. The average tenure of a federal departmental secretary is about three years. The average high-level government employee stays in the same department quite a bit longer.[4] Longer length of service obviously affords the professionals a basis for power. But the political appointees are usually their superiors. Once again the department has a potential split in its role when preparing the budget.

CENTRAL BUDGET OFFICE

The only participant in the budget preparation game that is involved on practically a full-time basis is the central budget office. This office is the staff agency to the chief executive for budgetary matters. As such it is probably the most influential control device at the executive's disposal. Through this agency the flow of money, the lifeblood of any operation, is controlled. Its crucial nature is manifest by its proximity to the chief executive in most jurisdictions. The essential and intimate relation between the chief executive and the director of the central budget office is illustrated by the fact that until very recently the director of the Office of Management and Budget was one of the few high-ranking policy-level officials in Washington appointed by the president without Senate approval.

The job of the central budget office is the preparation of the executive branch's budget requests, which are frequently called estimates. In one sense this is a rather routine and mundane responsibility, almost clerical in nature. Some degree of uniformity must be imposed on the format of the requests submitted by the sources of agencies for hundreds of activities. And the paperwork regarding the requests must be collated and organized so that a budget document can be compiled for presentation to the legislature. Historically this aspect of central budget control was preeminent. In some governmental jurisdictions the central budget office only issues instructions on how budget requests are to be made, what kind of documentation must accompany the requests, and puts together a document.

The clerical aspects of a central budget office's activities have generally been superceded in importance by its policy-making duties. In Washington this was manifested by moving the Bureau of the Budget (BOB) from the Treasury Department to the newly created Executive Office of the President in 1939. In 1970 BOB was reorganized into the Office of Management and Budget (OMB) and so was supposedly to get more deeply involved in the daily managerial aspects of the executive branch. This shift in focus is easily understandable given the increasing size of the executive establishment and the necessity that the chief executive devote him or herself to constantly arising crises. While the chief executive is involved in the crisis of the day, someone must be "watching the store" to make sure that agencies are doing what the chief executive wants them to do. This is one job of the central budget office.

The typical organization of a central budget office allows chief executives both to find out what is going on at the agency and program level and to implement their policy preferences. Basic to central budget offices are the budget examiners, also called budget analysts, policy advisors, and similar-sounding names. Each examiner is assigned an agency or usually a group of agencies. It is that person's responsibility to assist the line or operating agency in preparation of budget requests that are in accordance with the policies set by the chief executive officer.

The central budget office really has only one client or supporter — the chief executive officer. As his or her eyes and ears in the agencies, they purvey the official policies, which often times are not what the agency personnel want to hear. In fact they have been called "abominable no-men." Consequently they may not have many fans in the line agencies.

The orientation of central budget office personnel is usually fiscal in view of what they have to do.[5] Because there are insufficient funds to give every agency all that it wants, the budget analysts must insist that agencies cut back their requests to fall within the ceilings set by the chief executives. Because of the close relationship between the director of the budget office and the chief executive, budget office personnel generally have a good idea of what kinds of programs are favored by the chief executive and what kinds are not. This information assists them in deciding where to reduce agency requests. Occasionally agency personnel do not accept the decisions of the budget office regarding their requests and bypass them, going to the chief executive for a final resolution.

Although agency personnel will view budget examiners as being dominated by a fiscal orientation because they usually seek to restrain attempts for expansion, budget examiners do, to some degree, become committed to specific programs. Constant contact with agency personnel in close proximity to agency programs can turn what should be a neutral and objective analyst into something of a supporter for some programs. L. L. Wade's interviews found that federal budget officials did not always adhere to a perfectly neutral stance with regard to programs.[6] To become completely trapped by agency personnel, however, makes budget analysts useless in their position.

The background of central budget office personnel is overwhelmingly professional. The director of the office and some immediate subordinates may be political appointees, but the bulk of those who actually exercise budget control and policy evaluation positions with regard to the agencies are civil service employees. In fact, budget office employees typically take pride in their neutrality. Were they to come typecast as being subject to partisan influence, their effectiveness and value to the chief executive would plummet. Chief executives want neutral advice so that they can add the political concerns.

The training of budget officers suggests their professional posture.[7] In the clerical days of BOB and other budget agencies those with accounting backgrounds formed the bulk of budget agency personnel. Later when management concerns became more salient, people with training in public administration and business administration were hired. Most recently, when program analysis and program evaluation have become the watch words, economic backgrounds have begun to characterize the people hired. In all of these cases, career civil servants with professional training, largely taken outside the agency, staff the central budget office. This all goes to ensure neutral and objective performance.

In summary, central budget office personnel, because they prosper only by serving the chief executive, provide neutral advice. They generally find themselves being the professional hair shirts, pointing out problems and limitations in programs. They are the hatchet men who enforce the fiscal constraints at the specific agency and program level.

All the budget preparation actors just presented interact in a largely sequential process. Each deals with others who are generally hierarchically superior to them. But this does not prevent each actor from presenting his or her case. The end result is a compromise, something that most participants can or must live with. That final result is then sent to the legislative body for modification and eventual approval.

THE BUDGET APPROVAL GAME: ACTORS AND ROLES

In approving the budget the prime sets of actors are executive branch officials on one side and the legislative branch personnel on the other. The initiative in this interaction lies with the executive branch actors because they present their estimates of what it would cost to execute the substantive programs the chief executive envisions.

From presentation of the budget document to the legislature onward the executive branch personnel tend to act in concert. Even though a few months or even weeks earlier there had been severe and widespread disagreement among agencies, departments, central budget officials, and the chief executive, once the budget goes to the legislature a common front is typically presented. Since the chief executive is held responsible for the actions of the entire executive branch, all subordinates are expected to fall in line. At the federal level, in fact, agency personnel are expected to ask only for what the president finally allowed them to request. Indeed, there are strong norms prohibiting the agency from telling Congress what its original request was to the department or what the department asked of OMB. In response to a direct request, of course, agency personnel must divulge such information. Because of this unity, in what follows the executive branch is considered as one rather unified actor, at least with regard to the budget requests.

In many states, however, the budget estimates of the agencies as well as the recommendations of the governor are made known to the legislature. This obviously allows state legislators to see where there was lack of agreement between agency and governor. While it appears that the governor's decision may not have been the binding one, research results presented later in this chapter show that in most cases the governor's decision is the most influential one.

The legislature in the approval process is not as unified as the executive branch in the preparation phase. There is, however, quite a bit of variation from one government jurisdiction to the next and consequently some legislatures are almost monolithic in comparison with others. The federal government is an example of the most specialized and least unified. There are two chambers, the House and the Senate; within each chamber there is an appropriations committee that has the responsibility to examine budget requests (now there is also a budget committee in each chamber, too). Within each appropriations committee there are numerous subcommittees that do most of the real work; and because there frequently are differences between House and Senate versions of appropriations bills, a conference committee often becomes involved in the process. At the opposite extreme would be the municipal council of a small to medium-sized city. There the council as a whole considers the budget presented by the mayor and makes all decisions acting by itself, often as a committee of the whole.

FEDERAL LEVEL

Because of its complexity, the federal budget approval actors and roles will be presented, and variations of this will be introduced along the line to differentiate that process and its participants from those at the state and local levels.

COMMITTEES.   Central to understanding legislators' behavior is a knowledge of the committee system. Because legislatures are called upon to make wise decisions on a range of questions, some very technical, they tend to specialize their membership. Each group or committee is devoted to a particular topic, such as agriculture, merchant marine and fisheries, defense, nuclear energy, or appropriations. By restricting their energies to one or a few topics, legislators can theoretically become expert in some field. To take advantage of the expertise thus available, whenever legislation dealing with a specific topic is introduced, it is referred to the specialist committee, which renders its opinion on the matter to the entire chamber in the form of a report. The entire chamber then seriously considers the opinions of the "experts" in making their collective decision. When the entire legislature makes its decision, non-technical and nonspecialist criteria are sure to be brought into play. Legislatures are, after all, representative bodies and the goals and values of the diverse population are sure to be brought up. The difference between the more or less specialized and expert opinions coming from the committees and the more general and popular opinions coming from the entire body of the legislature forms one of the sources of divergence in the legislature during the approval phase. Keeping all this in mind, the role of the general legislator is first discussed.

The reference, support, or constituent groups a legislator faces are highly influential in explaining appropriations behavior. Consider the chamber as a whole and take the average legislator. His or her prime support groups are comprised of the folks back home who elected the legislator to office. To stay in office, which is a prime goal, the legislator must please the people back in the district by either giving them what they want or by making them think their representative is doing that. What does the average citizen want? Low taxes are clearly desired by all citizens, no matter what their district. Just as clearly, but perhaps harder to generalize about, everyone wants the tax money collected to be spent back in the home district.

The nature of the constituency the average legislator responds to readily explains the orientation of most legislators toward appropriations matters. Since most appropriations bills do not obviously affect the congressperson's district, the fiscal orientation is the most congenial. Without information to the contrary, legislators are inclined to support cutting money from an agency's request. If, however, it is brought to their attention that a particular agency's request would benefit the constituents back home, legislators would undoubtedly support the request and thereby take a selectively programmatic orientation.

What was said earlier about the politically appointed executive branch officials applies also to legislators. Their background is usually not technical. Most have held elected office before the national legislature and the overwhelming majority of them are attorneys. Thus they are political in background. A major difference between the behavior of executive and legislative branch politicos is that the element of partisanship operates very overtly on the floor of the legislature in passing appropriation bills but has little influence in the formulation of budget requests — largely because most executive branch politicos are all of the same party.

The role of the average legislator in appropriations matters will most likely be constituency directed, primarily fiscally oriented, and influenced by partisan political considerations. At the national level, while the average senator and the average representative will generally conform to the same role, because of a difference in the size of the constituencies served, there will be some difference in orientation between the two houses. The average congressional district has under a half-million people in it while the average state or senatorial district has many times that number of people. The increased size almost invariably means greater heterogeneity of interests. Thus more agency programs are likely to benefit the average senator's constituents and the Senate therefore tends to be less fiscally conservative than the House. Additionally, because senators have longer terms of office, they can advocate higher spending without fear of immediate ouster from the legislature. Since the House generally votes on appropriations bills before the Senate, the upper chamber has in the past acted as an appeals court, raising the amount of money appropriated by the House.

The next group to be discussed is the appropriations committee. While they share all the characteristics of the average legislator just dealt with, there are some crucial differences. For one, not only do all committee members feel the pressures of the constituents in their home districts, but the appropriations committee has its entire legislative chamber as its constituency. The chamber as a whole expects the committee to behave in certain ways and to safeguard certain values. To be specific, an appropriations committee is expected to guard the public purse, to see to it that spending is kept down. Additionally, the committee will be exposed to the parochial desires of individual legislators to find programs that will benefit their districts. The economizing expectation will usually be the more dominant expectation. Thus, because of the committee's legislative constituency, its orientation will be primarily fiscal.

Because of its specialized function, the appropriations committee will often move away from a purely political role to manifest some degree of professionalism. To be sure, this professionalism or expertise is not the result of outside schooling; but by virtue of constant exposure to questions of agency activity and the funding necessary for various programs, a degree of professionalization becomes apparent. This expertise is used by the committee to get the agreement or at least acquiescence of the entire chamber to the committee's recommendations. This specialization also serves as a protective device by means of which the committee can justify not giving in to demands of legislators to allocate money for their pet projects. Political wisdom, of course, demands that the committee give in to some of these particularistic demands on occasion. In general, however, it is to the benefit of the committee to emphasize its neutral and professional reputation inasmuch as this allows the committee maximal freedom.

Legislative committees in general try to make their reports unanimous because any show of division in a specialist committee indicates to the chamber as a whole that the "experts" are not in agreement and so the matter is not fixed. Floor amendments and debate therefore can change the committee recommendations. For appropriations committees in Congress unanimity in recommendations is usually the case. These members of Congress, working in one of the most prestigious committees, generally leave partisanship and divisiveness behind them and so can present a united and therefore authoritative front to their respective chambers.[8] Because of the unity and hardworking reputation of congressional appropriations committees, their recommendations are generally the real decisions in allocating funds, and the chamber as a whole basically ratifies decisions made in committee.

SUBCOMMITTEES.   In large legislatures the real locus of decision making lies not in committees but in subcommittees. The logic of specialization dictates that if one group devoted to a particular function — spending — can make better decisions than the undifferentiated parent group, then, should the committee specialize into subcommittees, each expert on a particular area of spending, decisions made in the subcommittees will be doubly enlightened. In the federal government most decisions are really made in appropriations subcommittees. Hearings on the appropriations bill actually take place before subcommittees and their reports are presented by the whole committee.

Subcommittees, and the entire committee in smaller units of government, become the most professionally oriented group in the legislature. This comes about because of long contact with the same agencies and the same clients of the agencies. In fact, a triangle of mutual interests often develops among agencies, their clients, and the appropriations decisional unit in the legislature. Clients want to receive services from agencies. But agencies need money that only legislatures can bestow. Consequently, clients will urge legislators to appropriate for "their agencies." Legislators, on the other hand, want votes, which will be forthcoming if clients are happy. And agencies are willing to make clients happy if they have the resources to do so. This mutality of interests guarantees that information about needs, programs, and financing is exchanged in the triangle, which enhances the professionalism of the subcommittee or committee members.

The interaction between agencies, clients, and subcommittee members means that the subcommittee gains another reference or support group in addition to the legislature as a whole. Familiarity does not always breed contempt if the experience of congressional appropriations subcommittees is any indication. Legislators involved in appropriations often become ensnared by the programs and agencies they oversee and develop into advocates of the very agencies their legislative peers expect them to scrutinize severely and keep operating frugally. Representative John Fogarty of the House Appropriations Committee is an excellent example of a legislator whose reference, support, or client group in matters of health research became the agencies doing the research rather than the economically oriented legislature funding the research. The orientation, in some policy areas at least, thus becomes more programmatic than fiscal.

CONFERENCE COMMITTEES.   The last legislative actor considered here is the conference committee in bicameral legislatures. It was noted that senators tend to be more liberal than representatives because of broader constituencies and longer terms. Consequently, the version of the appropriations bill reported out of the House will often be less than the version espoused by the Senate. Whenever two versions of the same bill are passed, differences must be ironed out before the bill can be sent to the chief executive for signature. In the appropriations process the most senior members of the committees in both houses that worked on the bill are appointed to the conference committee that prepares a compromise bill for consideration by both houses. The reference, client, or support groups for this committee are the two houses. They expect a version of the bill that they can live with. These expectations draw upon the political skills of the conferees to generate an acceptable compromise on all items in dispute. Because these committees typically operate in secrecy with no records kept, little is known about regularities in how decisions are made.

STATE AND MUNICIPAL LEVELS
The presentation just made of the legislative actors and their roles was based heavily on the federal case. Obviously there will be variation from that situation at other governmental levels. At the state level, for example, most of the activity will probably take place in the appropriations committee as a whole. But probably the most crucial difference between the state and federal levels is the degree of professionalism. Professionalism when applied to the legislature refers to the expertise developed from experience and continued contact between the legislators on the one hand and the agencies and

their clients on the other. Professionalism so defined is inhibited from developing in many states because of the rapid turnover in the legislatures. Compared
to Congress, where turnover is relatively low, the states are faced with legislatures that constantly have a large proportion of new faces. Even when a state
legislature retains a good number of people, it frequently is the case that they
cannot maintain the constant contact with agencies and their programs because
the legislator's position is part-time — the legislature only meets for a fixed
number of days every year or every other year — or legislators lack the staff
assistance necessary to perform an adequate job. In at least one state legislators
have only their desks on the floor of the capitol building for working. When
professionalism or resources is lacking, the role of the legislator is more likely
to become increasingly fiscal because little or no information is available to
discriminate among programs to decide where and how to modify the executive's request.

At the municipal level the same problems or characteristics facing state
legislatures appear. Council members are almost invariably part-time. Staff
assistance is generally minimal and specialization tends not to become institu-
tionalized. The only mitigating circumstance that allows some degree of programmatic orientation or professionalism to develop is the smaller scale of
operations in most municipalities. Overall, though, the role of legislators in
the appropriations process is characterized by high concern for an electoral
constituency, which usually translates into a fiscal, economizing orientation
except when the electoral constituents would benefit by higher spending levels.
Moreover, given the need to balance conflicting interests, political rather than
professional background and concerns dictate most behavior.

OUTCOMES IN THE BUDGETARY PROCESS

Even though the roles assumed by the various participants in the budget
process are quite varied, with each participant having a different configuration
of support or constituency groups, orientation, and professionalization, conflict
among them is not unrestrained. In fact the interaction is usually quite civilized.
Conflict is reduced largely because the entire process is sequential and any
participant is generally dealing with one other participant at a time. Moreover
there is a kind of moving finality in the process in that a decision made by
one set of actors at one stage is taken as given by the next set of actors.

Only in the differences between versions of appropriations bills from the two chambers is there a reworking of previous decisions. Even there the points of disagreement are quite few in comparison with the vast number of agreements. Conflict, however, does occur and the resolution of that conflict is not foreordained in any particular case.

Given that there are relatively stable roles and given that the interaction is routinized, some regularities in the outcomes of the budgetary game are to be expected. In this section data are presented that illustrate the behavior of the participants and that support the contention that these outcomes are understandable, if not crudely predictable, on the basis of the roles and rules found in the budget "game."

Table 4.1 displays data showing the budget formulation stages for bureaus in the U.S. Department of Labor for fiscal year 1967. The base point for each agency is its previous year's appropriation, in this case the appropriation for FY1966. The estimates or requests made by the bureaus to the Department of Labor are, with only two exceptions, for more money than they had already been appropriated. This is to be expected inasmuch as the agency orientation is usually one of programmatic enhancement. Note that the bureaus ask for a reasonable increase but not outlandish amounts; no agency tries to double its size.

The department's actions on agencies' requests reflect a fiscal orientation inasmuch as it cuts the requests. But it is instructive to note that eight of the twenty-two appropriations items were untouched. This reflects the programmatic orientation of the department. While it must cut some requests, it leaves some unscathed. The decisions made by the Budget Bureau as indicated in the column "President's Budget" demonstrate a cutting or fiscal orientation because seventeen of the twenty-two items are cut below what the department allowed. Although the department removed $112 million from the agencies' requests, the Budget Bureau trimmed a further $178 million from the department's figures. Yet fifteen of the twenty-two agencies were allowed to ask for more money than they had. This is either a recognition of the need to meet inflation and similar forces or approval of some program enhancement.

The data just presented and discussed is not atypical of what happens in the budget formulation process. Table 4.2 displays the mean percentage increase sought by selected Labor Department agencies for a ten-year period in the late 1950s and 1960s. In general the Labor Department reduced the agencies' requests by a small amount and the Bureau of the Budget did the same

TABLE 4.1. BUDGET FORMULATION, DEPARTMENT OF LABOR, FY1967, COMPARISON OF BUREAU REQUESTS WITH DEPARTMENTAL APPROVAL AND BUREAU OF BUDGET ACTION.

BUREAU	1966 APPROPRIATION	ESTIMATE TO DEPARTMENT	1967		
			DEPARTMENT ESTIMATE TO BUDGET BUREAU	ESTIMATE TO BUDGET BUREAU	PRESIDENT'S BUDGET
Manpower Development and Training activities	$399,595,000	$512,900,000	$512,900,000		$400,044,000
Office of Manpower Administrator	35,410,800	52,966,100	52,955,100		39,162,000
Admission and employment of immigrant and nonimmigrant aliens	1,723,000	2,000,000	2,000,000		
Civil rights		536,000	536,000		
Trade adjustment activities (Automotive Products Trade Act)	10,000,000	9,730,000	9,730,000		
Bureau of Apprenticeship and Training	7,105,000	8,760,400	8,670,850		8,397,000
Grants to states	492,100,000	504,450,000	504,450,000		508,950,000
Advances for employment services	10,000,000	144,952,000	63,302,000		23,000,000
Unemployment compensation for federal employees & ex-servicemen	118,896,100[a]	131,000,000	107,000,000		107,000,000
Bureau of Employment Security salaries and expenses	19,466,200	22,895,700	21,109,700		22,009,000
Labor Management Service Administration	8,580,000	8,652,000	8,600,000		8,510,000
Wage and Hour Division	21,519,000	23,819,700	23,618,900		22,256,000

Bureau of Labor Standards	3,281,500	5,285,600	4,195,500	3,349,000
Women's Bureau	871,000	1,018,265	1,018,265	888,000
Bureau of Employees' Compensation				
Salaries and Expenses	4,617,550	4,839,700	4,829,700	4,772,000
Compensation Fund	48,530,000	44,375,000	44,375,000	44,375,000
Bureau of Labor Statistics	19,968,000	24,438,700	22,072,700	20,785,000
Bureau of Int'l. Labor Affairs	1,219,000	1,667,000	1,365,000	1,230,000
Office of Solicitor	5,608,000	6,116,700	5,903,700	5,591,000
Office of the Secretary	3,720,000	4,128,300	3,954,700	3,825,000
Office of Federal Contract Compliance	451,000	710,200	710,200	689,000
President's Committee Consumer Interests				327,000
TOTAL	1,212,661,150	1,515,241,365	1,403,297,315	1,225,159,000

SOURCE: U.S. Congress, House, Appropriations Committee, *Hearings on Department of Labor and Health, Education and Welfare for FY1967*, Part 1, p. 156.

a. Excludes any 1966 carryover balances.

TABLE 4.2. MEANS OF INDICES MEASURING INTERACTION IN BUDGET FORMULATION IN THE U.S. DEPARTMENT OF LABOR, FY1959–1968.

AGENCY	% INCREASE SOUGHT BY AGENCY OVER PREVIOUS AP-PROPRIATION	% INCREASE ALLOWED BY DEPT. OF LABOR	% OF LABOR DEPT. ALLOW-ANCE APPROVED BY BUDGET BUREAU
Bureau of Apprenticeship and Training	21.99%	91.88%	97.09%
Office of the Secretary of Labor	31.78	96.01	92.45
Office of the Solicitor	20.93	97.45	94.42
Bureau of Labor Statistics	37.51	91.12	94.37
Bureau of Labor Standards	54.48	89.78	93.57
Bureau of Employment Security	32.93	92.53	96.78
Wage and Hour Division	16.25	95.98	95.97
Women's Bureau	28.21	89.64	93.68
Consumer Price Index Revision	120.55	100.00	98.63

SOURCE: U.S., Congress, House, Appropriations Committee, *Hearings on the Departments of Labor and Health, Education and Welfare* for fiscal years 1959 through 1968, various pages.

to the figures proposed by the department. Except for revising the Consumer Price Index, moderation appears to be the watchword.

In the most comprehensive study of the budgetary process in the federal government to date, Richard Fenno examined 36 domestic bureaus in the period from 1947 to 1962. Out of 576 agency requests he found that 80.9 percent of the requests were for more than their previous appropriation, 3.5 percent sought the same appropriation, and 15.8 percent asked for less money than they presently had.[9] The data from the Labor Department presented in the previous tables is therefore in line with the findings of Fenno's broader study.

While agency averages in table 4.2 generally appear to be in the same range, the differences are instructive. The Bureau of Labor Standards is much more aggressive in seeking funds than the Wage and Hour Division. The Bureau of Labor Standards, however, is not treated well by either the department or the Bureau of the Budget. The Bureau of Employment Security and the Bureau of Apprenticeship and Training, on the other hand, are treated relatively well by the Budget Bureau but not by the department. Such variation has to be attributable to specific configurations of clients, programs, and interpersonal skills characteristic of the agencies and their personnel.

The behavior of Congress in the appropriations process is what the role analysis leads one to believe. Table 4.3 presents the experience of the Department of Labor's Manpower Administration training activities from fiscal year 1963 through fiscal year 1971. Each year the president's request for training activities exceeded the previous year's appropriation, as one would expect from the discussion above. The House allowance in two years was what the agency requested, but in the remaining seven years the House cut into the agency request. The Senate agreed with the House in one year, cut the request below the House figure in two years, but approved an appropriation higher than the House's in six years. In all cases the final appropriation was less than or equal to the president's request for manpower training activities but, with one exception, was also greater than the appropriation for the previous year.

The pattern appearing in the history shown in table 4.3 certainly conforms to expectations. The House, being heavily economy oriented, cut the agency requests to satisfy the expectations of its constituencies. The Senate, having more of a programmatic or at least less of a fiscal orientation, cut less deeply into the agencies' requests. In fact, there are years in which the Senate proposed to give the agency more money than the president asked for. The final appropriation varied in relation to the actions of the two chambers, which is what one expects from the heavily political approach that must be used by conferees in the conference committee.

Once again the Labor Department data in table 4.3 is congruent with the

TABLE 4.3. MANPOWER ADMINISTRATION MANPOWER TRAINING ACTIVITIES APPROPRIATIONS HISTORY.

YEAR	ESTIMATE TO OFFICE OF MANAGEMENT & BUDGET	BUDGET ESTIMATE TO CONGRESS	HOUSE ALLOWANCE	SENATE ALLOWANCE	APPROPRIATION
1963	$100,155,000	$100,155,000	147,250	$75,147,250	$70,147,250
1964	165,522,000	165,000,000	140,000,000	134,300,000	130,000,000
1965	411,000,000	411,000,000	402,906,000	412,906,000	396,906,000
1966	398,478,900	399,595,000	399,595,000	399,595,000	399,595,000
1967	512,955,000	400,044,000	400,044,000	390,044,000	390,044,000
1968	588,939,400	401,854,000	394,997,000	460,497,000	398,497,000
1969	497,678,000	413,088,000	399,992,000	409,992,000	407,492,000
1970[a]	1,883,488,000	1,536,615,000	670,815,000	1,586,615,000	1,451,215,000
1971[a]	1,580,644,000	1,548,944,000	1,504,044,000	1,558,644,000	1,516,744,000

SOURCE: U.S., Congress, House, Appropriations Committee, *Hearings on Departments of Labor and Health Education and Welfare for 1972*, Part 5, p. 110.
a. Data for Fiscal Years 1970 and 1971 adjusted on a comparative basis.

older but more comprehensive study of Richard Fenno. He found, for instance, that 92 percent of the House Appropriations Committee decisions were to cut or allow the agency its request; only 18.4 percent of the requests were granted.[10] But when there was a cut, it usually was not a very big one. As an indication of this behavior he found that 52.2 percent of all the agency requests were cut less than 10 percent.[11]

Comparing the House committee action with the agency's previous appropriation shows that although the fiscal orientation predominated, the agencies were still allowed to grow. For example, 73 percent of the House Appropriations Committee actions allowed the agency to get the same or more than they had been appropriated in the previous year.[12] The growth allowed, however, was not great. The House committee allowed between a zero and 10 percent growth 34.4 percent of the time, allowed between a 10 percent and 20 percent growth 17 percent of the time, and allowed between 20 percent and 30 percent growth 8 percent of the time.[13]

The expectation that the House as a whole would defer to the expertise represented by the House Appropriations Committee is also borne out by Fenno's data. In 89.9 percent of the cases the House accepted the committee's recommendation, in 5.2 percent of the cases it decreased the amount, and in 4.9 percent of the cases it increased it.[14] The changes, however, were usually made with the agreement of the bipartisan appropriations committee. No amendment to a House appropriations bill as reported out of committee was rejected if it had the committee's support and only six of sixty amendments opposed by the committee passed.[15]

Similar behavior was found in the Senate by Fenno; but there were some important differences, again probably attributable to the lesser degree of professionalism or expertise and the more diverse support groups. For instance, while the House Appropriations Committee recommended an increase over the agency request in only 8 percent of the cases, the Senate committee did so in 18.9 percent of the cases.[16] Similarly, while the House committee recommended that the agencies' requests be less than their previous appropriation in 27 percent of the cases, the Senate did this in only 22.4 percent of the cases.[17] The Senate's liberality, compared to the House, is further manifest by the fact that the Senate committee recommended a figure over the House's recommendation in 56.2 percent of the cases; they concurred in 33.6 percent of the requests.[18] However, the differences were small. In 75.1 percent of the requests, the House and Senate committee differed by less than 6 percent.[19]

Although the Senate as a whole tended to accept the recommendations of the Senate Appropriations Committee, it tended to raise the committee's recommendations when it did not accept them. In 8.9 percent of the cases the Senate increased the committee's recommendation.[20] The comparable figure for the House cited earlier was 4.9 percent.

At the state level there is less systematic evidence than at the federal level to verify the patterns predicted by the roles described above. But where it exists, the data does corroborate the expectations, as Sharkansky's study of budget relations among agencies, the governors, and the legislatures in nineteen states showed.[21] The agencies' programmatic or expansionary behavior was shown by their moderate but universal desires for increases in appropriations. The governors, who had to present a balanced budget, always recommended less money than the agencies desired. The legislatures also appropriated less money than the agencies wanted, but the agencies still managed to grow over the previous year's appropriation.

Overall, the roles assumed by the budget actors and the outcomes of the game yield a relatively happy and nondivisive ending. Conflict is minimized by the sequential nature of the process and by the process of marginal changes in successive stages. Everyone can claim some success and satisfy some of their support and client groups. Agencies, for example, do not get all they want, but in general they grow and can please their clients. Legislators can tell their general constituents in the electoral district and their peers in the legislature that they have cut back the agencies' drives for expansion. At the same time, because some expansion is allowed, legislators can reap the benefit of claiming credit for tangible programs serving special clients.

Of course, the statements above are all generalizations. In the specifics, some agencies do better than others; some subcommittees can cut more than others; some allow more expansion than others. Some chief executives see more of their budget proposals enacted than others. And there is variation from one year to another. The variation is explicable not in terms of general orientations, background, or expertise, but more specific and idiosyncratic factors. To make general explanations of general patterns, the substance of this chapter should suffice. To make more particular explanations or predictions, the reader is directed to chapter VII, where more specific theories, hypotheses, and studies are discussed.

SUMMARY

The explanation of budget behavior can be assisted by understanding the roles assumed by budget participants. Roles are strongly influenced in the budget process by the nature of the constituency, the fiscal or programmatic orientation, and the professional or political outlook of the participants.

Agencies are characterized by professional personnel with a strong programmatic orientation based on a specific constituency. They consequently seek budget expansion. Chief executives, serving broad constituencies and usually coming from political backgrounds, must balance conservative fiscal demands with programmatic priorities of their own. Consequently they both allow and seek higher funding levels for some agencies but also have to cut back on the desires of others. Department personnel must act to meet the programmatic demands of the agencies and also to meet the financial revenue constraints imposed on them by higher officials. Because department personnel have both political and professional backgrounds as well as diverse constituents inside and outside of government, their budgetary stance is variable. One of the least ambiguous roles is that of the central budget office personnel. They have one constituent, the chief executive officer, and must take on that person's balancing of programmatic and fiscal concerns. By background they are generally professionals. Revenue specialists are fiscally oriented; from professional backgrounds; and, like central budget office personnel, serve only one constituent, the chief executive officer.

In the budget approval phase, action by legislators is also made more understandable by consideration of their constiuency, background, and fiscal programmatic orientation. In general, legislators are dominated by their general constituency, which seeks reduced spending unless it offers an advantage to them. As politicians they will generally attempt to please their constituency, whatever it is asking for. The constituency of members of the appropriations committees are the rest of the legislators. They, too, seek low levels of spending unless the programs would benefit them or their constituencies. Budget action by legislators tends, then, to find resolution by allowing some increase over what the agencies were allowed to spend in the previous year, yet not as much as they had asked for.

NOTES

1. Some evidence exists that agencies do exhibit behavior that can be interpreted as fiscal in character although that behavior is muted compared to their programmatic characteristics. See John Wanat, "Bureaucratic Politics in the Budget Formulation Arena," *Administration and Society* 7 (August 1975): 191–212.

2. Frederick C. Mosher, *Democracy and the Public Service* (New York: Oxford University Press, 1968), p. 103.

3. A good description of forecasting at the federal level is found in Lawrence C. Pierce, *The Politics of Fiscal Policy Formulation* (Pacific Palisades, California: Goodyear Publishing, 1971), chapter 3.

4. See, for example, Michael Cohen, "The Generalist and Organizational Mobility," *Public Administration Review* 30 (September/October 1970), pp. 544–552; David T. Stanley, *The Higher Civil Service* (Washington, D.C.: The Brookings Institution, 1964), pp. 31–34.

5. Some programmatic concerns are inferred from data analyzed in Wanat.

6. L. L. Wade, "The U.S. Bureau of the Budget as Agency Evaluator: Orientations to Action," *American Journal of Economics and Sociology* 27 (1968): 55–62.

7. See the discussion in Allen Schick, "The Road to PPB: The Stages of Budget Reform," *Public Administration Review* 26 (December 1966): 243–258.

8. Richard F. Fenno, Jr., "The House Appropriations Committee as a Political System: The Problem of Integration," *American Political Science Review* 56 (June 1962): 310–324.

9. Richard F. Fenno, Jr., *The Power of the Purse* (Boston: Little, Brown, 1966), p. 267.

10. Ibid., p. 353.

11. Ibid.

12. Ibid., p. 355.

13. Ibid., p. 356.

14. Ibid., p. 450.

15. Ibid., p. 463.

16. Ibid., p. 573.

17. Ibid.

18. Ibid., p. 575.

19. Ibid., p. 578.

20. Ibid., p. 597.

21. Ira Sharkansky, "Agency Requests, Gubernatorial Support, and Budget Success in State Legislatures," *American Political Science Review* 62 (December 1968): 1220–1231.

SELECTED BIBLIOGRAPHY

Cohen, Michael. "The Generalist and Organizational Mobility." *Public Administration Review* 30 (September/October 1970): 544–552.

Davis, James W., and Ripley, Randall B. "The Bureau of the Budget and Executive Branch Agencies: Notes on Their Interaction." *Journal of Politics* 29 (November 1967): 749–769.

Fenno, Richard F., Jr. "The House Appropriations Committee as a Political System: The Problem of Integration." *American Political Science Review* 56 (June 1962): 310–324.

_____. *The Power of the Purse: Appropriations Politics in Congress.* Boston: Little, Brown, 1966.

Harris, Joseph. "The General Accounting Office: Functions and Issues." In *Congressional Control of Administration,* edited by Joseph Harris. Washington, D.C.: The Brookings Institution, 1964.

Heclo, Hugh. "OMB and the Presidency." *Public Interest* 38 (Winter 1975): 80–98.

Horn, Stephen. *Unused Power: The Work of the Senate Committee on Appropriations.* Washington, D.C.: The Brookings Institution, 1970.

Mosher, Frederick C. *Bureaucracy and the Public Service.* New York: Oxford University Press, 1968.

Pierce, Lawrence C. *The Politics of Fiscal Policy Formation.* Pacific Palisades, California: Goodyear Publishing, 1971.

Schick, Allen. "The Budget Bureau That Was: Thoughts on the Rise, Decline and Future of a Presidential Agency." *Law and Contemporary Problems* 35 (Summer 1970): 519–539.

_____. "The Road to PPB: The Stages of Budget Reform." *Public Administration Review* 26 (December 1966): 243–258.

Sharkansky, Ira. "Agency Requests, Gubernatorial Support, and Budget Success in State Legislatures." *American Political Science Review* 62 (December 1968): 1220–1231.

_____. "An Appropriations Subcommittee and Its Client Agencies." *American Political Science Review* 59 (September 1965): 622–628.

_____. "Four Agencies and an Appropriations Subcommittee: A Comparative Study of Budget Strategies." *Midwest Journal of Political Science* 9 (August 1965): 254–281.

Stanley, David T. *The Higher Civil Service.* Washington, D.C.: The Brookings Institution, 1964.

Wade. L. L. "The U.S. Bureau of the Budget as Agency Evaluator: Orientations to Action." *American Journal of Economics and Sociology* 27 (1968): 55–62.

Wanat, John. "Bureaucratic Politics in the Budget Formulation Arena." *Administration and Society* 7 (August 1975): 191–212.

Chapter V

BUDGET AS DOCUMENTS
        AND TECHNICAL TOOLS:

The Impact

of Budget Type

B efore any agency of the executive branch can spend money in pursuit of its goals, that money must be appropriated by the legislature of the relevant governmental jurisdiction. Since legislatures typically do not know the details of most programs, they rely on the agencies to present them with requests for specific amounts of money. Those lists and the supporting material comprise the **budget document.** The budgets, as the documents are often called, are the subject of this chapter.

At a minimum, budgets are used to present in some detail the requests made by all the agencies of the executive branch as well as the requests of the judiciary and legislature. Obviously the ways in which one could break down an agency's needs for the coming year are limited only by the ingenuity of the agency personnel. There are, however, three major categorizations or budget formats commonly used in this country. Each of these is described, along with an analysis of the advantages, disadvantages, and particular characteristics of each budget type.

One must not get the impression that budget documents function solely to present requests for funding to the legislators responsible for overseeing government spending. Budgets also can be used to assist in the internal management processes of agencies. They can be used to plan for the future. They can be used for public relations purposes. It will become clear that the variety in budget types just alluded to is a consequence of the differing purposes that budgets can serve. The study of budget types consequently allows analysis of a number of facets of organizational behavior.

The change from one budget type to another, or just the modification of a budget process or budget type, permits an analysis of organizational change in general and organizational innovation in particular. In the last three to four decades two major budget reforms have been attempted across the country. The history of these attempts, successes and failures, provides information that will be useful in assessing the likely success of ongoing and future attempts at budget reform.

In what follows, therefore, the practically oriented reader will garner information on the kinds of budgets and the uses to which they can be put. The more theoretically or politically oriented reader can gather data regarding governmental change and reform.

BUDGET MECHANICS

No matter what kind of budget a governmental unit employs, it will at least be presented to the legislature as the basis for the legislators' deliberations on what should be appropriated. Because the document is used by legislators, certain elements will be common in almost all jurisdictions.

For one, the spending agency is generally the basic unit of budget presentation, the dominant organizing category. Appropriations statutes typically are nothing but lists of agencies and the amount of money each is allowed to spend. The reproduction in the appendix of a portion of a Department of Labor and Department of Health, Education and Welfare appropriations bill (document 5) illustrates this point. Because the final decision legislators make is aggregated to the agency level, budget documents are geared to that level. The presentation of requests may be more detailed or refined within the agency in the budget document or they may have similar programs and activities grouped together. But at some point agency-by-agency-level requests are usually presented.

A second element common to all budgets is the presentation of appropriations data for at least three years. Budgets always indicate how much money had been appropriated for the past fiscal year, how much has been appropriated so far for the present fiscal year, and how much is being requested or estimated for the fiscal year under consideration. Thus, if the budget is for fiscal year 1978–79, the last column in most displays would have the amounts being requested for, say, the activities of a particular agency. A column to the left of that would list the amounts appropriated for activities in FY1977–78, and the first column would detail the money appropriated for FY1976–77. In large part this multiyear data presentation is to assist legislators in making comparisons between spending levels from one year to the next.

In some budgets data are presented for more than three years. A number of states have biennial legislative sessions, which means that budgets must cover a two-year period. Even though money is appropriated for two-year periods, the budget generally breaks the biennium into one-year periods. A typical budget for the biennium FY1978–80 would have two columns for the requests for each of the years in the 1978–80 biennium, two columns for the current appropriations of 1976–78, and two columns for the past biennium, 1974–76.

In a few jurisdictions where planning is emphasized the budget will list the past, the current, the requested, and the projected level of spending for a few years. The projected levels of spending are not binding on the agency but do serve to give the legislators an idea of the longer term implications of present budget levels. No matter what variant of budget document is presented, it will always present data on spending for at least the past, present, and next fiscal years.

Third, every budget contains the estimates of revenue for the fiscal year under consideration. While these estimates may not be what will actually come into the treasury, the estimates allow legislators to judge the wisdom of the proposed spending levels.

BUDGET TYPES

In what follows three major kinds of budget are presented.[1] A reproduction of a portion of an actual budget is displayed for each in the appendix. The physical format of the budget type is described in some detail. To help readers understand the uses of the budget more fully, the milieu generating the budget type is discussed. Finally, the relationship between the budget document and its use in the process described in the last chapters is elaborated.

The most prevalent budget types usually fall under the umbrella term "executive budget." This simply means that budget proposals are prepared by, approved by, and presented to the legislature by the chief executive. Prior to the twentieth century it was not at all uncommon for agencies and departments to deal directly with the appropriating body or bodies to get their funding. In its budgetary practices the executive branch was fragmented, decentralized, and practically anarchic. In times when the treasury is full, it is possible to tolerate the extravagance permitted and even encouraged by the lack of any central control. But when revenues are not sufficient to cover the fiscal aspirations of all the spending units acting independent of each other, some central coordinating mechanism is called for. Most often this is provided by requiring that all agency and department requests for funds be approved by the chief executive's central budget office.

Since chief executives are generally aware of revenue constraints, they are ideally able to put some outer limits on the spending desired by the agencies and departments. Moreover, the notions of accountability in democratic theory suggest that if chief executives are to be held responsible for their stewardship of the government, it is only reasonable that they have power over the executive branch's activities. This translates into central clearance of the spending units' aspirations for funds.

Since executives almost invariably have the responsibility for preparation of a document detailing the requests their agencies make to the legislature, in what follows it is assumed that all the budget types are executive budgets. There are exceptions, to be sure. Arkansas, for example, has a budget prepared by the legislature. The vast majority of governments in the United States, however, operate under some kind of executive budget. Attention is now turned to the varieties of executive budgets that are found in government.

THE OBJECT OF EXPENDITURE BUDGET

At the turn of the century two of the most salient concerns related to government spending were legality and economy. In the political life of this country political bosses and party machines dominated government. The excesses of political interference in the operation of what some reformers thought should be neutral administrative machinery brought about a demand for control over the politically tainted executive branch. One need only read George Washington Plunkitt's plain talks about practical politics to get the flavor of political involvement and intrusion into the supposedly neutral bureaucracy.[2] Chapter titles such as "Honest Graft and Dishonest Graft" and "The Curse of Civil Service Reform" indicate that legality was often flaunted at the time.

Similarly, the cost of government was becoming alarming. At the federal level up until the turn of the century the revenues from tariffs were generally more than adequate to cover the needs of government, to the point of regularly having surpluses in the treasury. This revenue source soon became inadequate to the demands placed upon it, which meant that new revenue sources had to be found, spending had to become less wasteful, or both.

In order to reduce the likelihood of excessive patronage and similarly costly partisan interferences in the neutral execution of the laws, as well as to guarantee more economical expenditure of the increasingly scarce revenues, two innovations were instituted in the budget mechanism. One was the executive budget alluded to earlier. Because the chief executive is head of the executive branch and will be held responsible for government spending, it is only logical to give him or her authority over agencies' desires for money. The creation of a central budget office gave the chief executive some control previously lacking. But while the establishment of an executive budget gave the legislature and citizenry a narrower focus point in their demands for prudence and economy in spending, a second innovation was more helpful.

The **object of expenditure budget** was an innovation that permitted control of spending to a degree that was previously unknown. Prior to its introduction budget requests were often made for a lump sum with little or no indication as to how the money would be spent. If the orientation of the reformers, the legislature, and the chief executive was to control spending and so reduce partisan intrusion and enhance economy, opening the proposed spending to scrutiny by detailing what the money was to purchase was a step in the right direction. Since all proposed expenditures were listed according to the objects for which money would be spent, this type of budget is commonly called an object of expenditure budget. It is occasionally referred to as a **line item budget** because each item of proposed expenditure is spelled out, a line to each item.

Document 6 in the appendix is a portion of a budget that provides an excellent example of a rather pure form of the object of expenditure budget. Note that for the agency under scrutiny all jobs are listed by title and by pay level. This information would be useful were one to try to weed out superfluous or overpaid personnel. Note also the detail of the accounting system permits identifying expenditures as small as a few dollars. Needless to say, breaking down an agency's requests for money to such a detailed level certainly facilitates control over spending.

The use of a uniform classification of objects of expenditure across agencies added to the multiyear data in the budget document allows comparisons both between agencies and across time. Overly large increases from one year to the next or from one agency to another stand out. The reviewer of the budget, be it an analyst from the central budget office, a chief executive, or a legislator, is afforded an opportunity to ask penetrating questions of the agency to force it to justify its requests. Accountability is mandated by disclosure of what an agency has and proposes to spend.

Even though the object of expenditure budget is heavily oriented to control, whether it is control by the chief executive over agencies or control by the legislature over the executive branch, other uses for the budget are still possible. To some degree this type of budget assists in managing an organization. The process of putting together a budget proposal requires analysis of one's needs, evaluation of what has been spent in the past, and some assessment of what is likely to be required in the future. Budget preparation, no matter what kind of budget it is, offers the opportunity for allowing the agency and oversight personnel to review operations and to plan for the future. The object of expenditure budget, however, does not offer an optimal vehicle for organizational self-analysis or planning.

The object of expenditure budget is probably the most common type found in operation today. Not all governmental units will have the same degree of detail or starkness of presentation that document 6 exemplifies, but virtually all budgets will have a breakdown indicating how much is proposed for salaries, for travel, for operating expenses, and for a number of other kinds of goods or services. Usually this object of expenditure data is presented in a more aggregated form than may have been common or necessary a few generations ago. Partly this is because the need for control is less today than before. The better quality of public employees, the higher standards of operation, and the greater expectation of neutral and competent service all reduce the need for control through detailed budgetary disclosures. Even where the need for control exists, nonbudgetary tools have developed or have become expanded in their use. To name but two, the expansion of civil service systems has reduced partisan intrusions in the form of patronage and open competitive bidding on contracts and purchases has minimized problems of "preferred" vendors.

THE PERFORMANCE BUDGET

No matter how requests are presented to the legislative oversight body, requests go to the legislature to guarantee some accountability of the governmental apparatus to the public. Accountability, however, can be focused in many directions. The object of expenditure budget seeks to foster legal accountability. But even though money is expended legally, it may not be expended efficiently. The performance budget aims to assist managers in wisely spending money in the sense that maximal output is achieved for minimal input. It is focused on efficiency accountability.

Ever since the New Deal, government has expanded greatly at all levels. Unfortunately, revenues have not always matched desired rates of spending. Yet expectations of government action and demands for government services have increased. If demands for government services increase while resources do not grow proportionately, the only solution is to use the resources more efficiently. Efficiency is usually defined as the ratio of the output to the input. Measuring efficiency therefore requires quantitative indications of both input and output. Because budgets are documents that present the inputs or costs in some detail, a budget is a good starting place for assessing the efficiency of governmental operations.

In a **performance budget** the focus is on the activities or the operations performed by the agency. Hence the classification scheme is not how much is spent on each object, but how much is spent on each activity. Instead of indicating that so much is spent on salaries, on utilities, on travel, on printing, on equipment, and so on, a performance budget would indicate that so much was spent on educational activities, on regulation, on research, and on executive direction. One hallmark of a performance budget document is the breakdown of spending by activities.

To assess efficiency truly there must be measurement of the activity. At the very least there have to be some kind of workload statistics such as the number of licenses issued, number of arrests made, number of checks issued, number of fires extinguished, number of meals served, and so on. Workload information alone permits some rather crude estimates of agency activity, particularly since budgets present data from at least three years. Comparison of workload data from agencies or branches of agencies performing much the same activity also allows rough indications of relative efficiency.

The best way to measure efficiency, however, is to utilize both workload data and cost data to determine the unit cost of activities. For example, efficiency would be gauged by the cost per license issued, the cost per arrest, the cost of issuing a check, the average cost of extinguishing a fire, the cost per meal served in the state hospital, and so on. Unit cost indicators compared over time or across agencies yield important information about whether an agency is becoming more or less efficient or which agency is operating more efficiently. Document 7 in the appendix illustrates the case of comparing unit cost data over time in a performance budget document. Similar data for other facilities permit evaluation of the efficiency of the various facilities.

As a managerial tool, a performance budget has great potential. Unfortunately, it is not equally applicable to all agencies. A regulatory operation can generate data on the number of inspections, the cost per inspection, and the number and cost per violation discovered. An agency promoting equal employment opportunity and civil rights or an agency involved in basic research does not have workload data that are as quantifiable. Even where quantifiable data are available they are not always meaningful. A state employment service can present data on cost per interview, per referral, per initial placement, and per long-term placement. Each of the indices measures a different activity and each measure has a different utility.

The ability to quantify an agency's activities puts definite limits on the usefulness of a performance budget for managerial purposes. State historical society executives would probably not be able to administer their operations more efficiently because of a performance budget. Such a budget, however, could be valuable in building or enhancing good relations with people outside of the agency, especially with legislators. Document 7 illustrates the fact that many performance budgets incorporate detailed description of the agency's mission and operation. A legislator considering a historical society request that describes what the agency aims to do and is doing will have more information and, it is hoped, more sympathy than one getting the same request in the stark object of expenditure format. Administrative officers and private citizens also can get more information out of a performance budget than out of an object of expenditure budget.

Although the performance budget has been contrasted with the object of expenditure budget, there really is no dichotomy. Examination of the budget in document 7 shows that this performance budget also has object of expenditure data built into it. While a **"pure" performance budget** could be characterized as having activity classifications, narratives, workload data, and unit cost measures, very few performance budgets would have only those earmarks. Most also include at least a breakdown of expenditures and requests according to the object of expenditure. Adoption of a performance budget has usually involved what Allen Schick calls hybridization.[3] That is to say, each governmental jurisdiction when dissatisfied with, say, an object of expenditure budget shifts to blending some variant of the old budget type with some elements of the new. This process of adaptation can prevent the full-fledged performance budget from becoming completely apparent in the budget document.

A distinction should be made at this point between a budget as a document and as a process. With the object of expenditure budget the document itself practically guaranteed the kind of budget process intended by its advocates. By forcing the agency personnel to present detailed requests in terms of objects, the agency personnel themselves became aware of the control that was intended. Chief executives and legislators when presented with the documents are almost immediately able to exert control by identifying questionable expenditures and by cutting requests. It is easy to say "reduce spending for travel" or "cut down on long distance telephone service" when everything is spelled out in terms of objects. Efficiency, however, is not guaranteed by presenting a document with unit cost data. Legislators and chief executives can use the document to point out problem areas or to identify wasteful agencies, but this does not itself increase efficiency.

A serious problem encountered in introducing any organizational change is goal displacement. In the introduction of a new type of budget the danger lies in the participants going through the motions and making the procedures the goals. Thus in the adoption of a performance budget, agency personnel may develop meaningless work measures simply because work measures are required by the budget office for inclusion in the budget document. Even if the work measures are germane to the mission of the organization, the budget preparation process may not be used as an occasion for evaluating the efficiency of the agency's operation. To make a performance budget fully operational, the agency personnel either have to think in terms of efficiency measures throughout the year and simply transfer this thinking to the document when it is being prepared or, less optimally, use the preparation process as a means to analyze agency operations. To the extent that performance budget documents are manifestations of agency operations and attitudes, one can speak of a successful budget adoption. Too often budget innovation is really a change in a document's format and not a change in the actual process of preparing a budget.

THE PROGRAM BUDGET

Budgets, it has been argued, at the very least are instruments to guarantee a minimal amount of accountability of bureaucracies to the oversight bodies, the legislatures, and through them to the ultimate repository of power, the citizenry. Accountability can be legal accountability, in which case an object of expenditure budget should be useful. Accountability can also be interpreted as managerial in nature, in which case the stewardship of program managers and their subordinates can be judged for efficiency by means of a performance budget. Yet another basic kind of accountability asks not if expenditure of government money is legal, economical, or efficient but asks if the expenditure is effective. Put bluntly, the real question is does the money spent by the agency achieve the desired results? Program budgets are a mechanism by which the question can be approached.

Program budgeting or a planning-programming-budgeting system (PPBS) is an attempt to use budget preparation as an occasion to evaluate rationally the programs an agency engages in so as to choose the programs most appropriate to the agency's goals. This budget type leaves some traces in the budget document, but the real action is found in the predocument stage. In terms of the documents versus process distinction introduced earlier, the program budget is really located in the process.

In the governmental sector program budgeting had its origins in the Department of Defense. The Army Corps of Engineers had to choose among many construction projects, each of which was proposed and supported by political figures. The Corps utilized a technique by which they evaluated the rival projects and so were able to judge which projects best achieved the goal of wise water resource management. This technique was not, however, explicitly tied to the budget process.

After the Second World War the military was faced with developing a series of weapons systems that would be adequate to the defensive and offensive demands placed on the United States. Put rather crudely, the kind of specific problem faced would be the following: Given a goal of being able to destroy a military objective of a certain size with a particular set of defenses located so many thousand miles away, should one invest in long-range missiles, strategic bomber forces, submarine-launched ballistic missiles, or what? Since each of the weapons systems has a particular complex of advantages and disadvantages, they had to be compared by some means. Since the weapons systems could not be bought over the counter, a longer time perspective had to be involved. That is, planning was essential. And because financing had to be procured for whatever system was selected, the entire endeavor had to be tied to the budget process. The PPBS is the name attached to the final process developed in the Defense Department.

Program budgeting has been applied to all sectors of the federal government, to many states, and to some local units of government. While there are many differences in the varieties of program budgets practiced, there are a number of basic similarities. Merewitz and Sosnick hold that **program budgets** are characterized by (1) a program classification system, (2) detailed narratives, (3) a multiyear time frame, (4) a zero base, and (5) the quantitative evaluation of alternatives.[4] Each of these is now briefly described.

As one might expect, the program classification system simply means that the budget document lists expenditures by programs. A health department, for example, could present its operations as a preventive health program, a regulation of health hazards programs, and a rehabilitative health program.

These in turn might be broken down into subprograms and program elements. Preventive health might be divided into health education programs and vaccination programs. The total amount of money for each program so spelled out in the budget document allows legislators and higher echelon administrators to see de facto priorities in the agency.

Detailed narratives in the document give explicit description of the programs. They serve to explain what the agency actually does and can serve to sell the program to the legislature.

The multiyear time frame illustrates the planning perspective of a program budget. Projecting the costs of programs past the next year makes it less likely that the long-term costs will unexpectedly appear. Oversight personnel are less likely to be surprised or presented with a fait accompli by agencies that tell them that a commitment made two years ago demands that so much be spent this next year. More rational choices are easier to make with this information.

The zero base characteristic of program budgets means that every year each program must be justified from the bottom up. Just because a program had been funded in the past does not mean that it deserves to be funded in the future. Since programs have often outlived their usefulness but are still continued, program goals frequently are not achieved. Zero-based budgeting increases the likelihood that dead wood will be culled out of operation. The zero base of budget preparation is not obvious from a budget document. It characterizes the preparation of the budget. Some analysts of budgeting, it should be noted, disagree with Merewitz and Sosnick by holding that zero-based budgeting is not part of PPBS. In fact, what is called **zero base budgeting** has by itself been touted in the mid-1970s as a budget innovation in its own right. Peter Phyrr initiated the zero base budget in the government sector in the state of Georgia and it has since been tried at the state level in at least New Jersey and New Mexico as of 1977.

Very briefly, the zero base budget procedures currently in vogue require that current and proposed agency activity be organized into decision packages that are ranked by the agency in order of importance relative to all other decision packages. The cost of each package is also estimated at various levels, for example, at the bare minimum level, at the current level, and at expanded levels. The rank ordering under total spending limits means that new programs compete with established programs, which suggests that no operation is sacrosanct. This fosters efficiency and effectiveness. The ranking of alternatives often requires analysis techniques central to PPB, to which attention is once again turned.

Probably the most central aspect of program budgeting is the quantitative assessment of alternatives. The major orientation of the program budget is effectiveness. Given a goal that the agency is to achieve, the agency is supposed to determine, within the context of the budget preparation, which alternative program would be the most effective. A housing agency given the problem of providing housing for, say, a hundred low-income families could approach the problem by proposing in the budget that public housing units be built or rent subsidies be given to the poor or mortgage guarantees be provided for low-cost housing, to name but three possibilities. For which alternative would the agency seek funding in its budget? By some cost effectiveness criterion each alternative is evaluated and the best one is selected.

A number of criteria is used to choose among the proposed alternatives. Each compares the benefits associated with each alternative to its costs. One criterion is the **benefit cost ratio,** which, as the name implies, is the ratio of the benefits accruing to a program alternative to its cost. Obviously the ratio must exceed one or the program does not even pay its way. Another criterion is the **net benefit,** defined as the excess of the benefit over the cost. Yet another criterion is the ratio of the marginal benefit to the marginal cost of a rank ordered set of alternatives. It is possible for one alternative to be chosen if the benefit cost ratio is employed and another alternative to be chosen if, say, the net benefit criterion is used. Since none of the criteria is graven in stone as being always and clearly superior to all the others, the rationality in choice that program budgeting promises can be illusory at times.

Assuming that there is agreement about the appropriate criterion to use, the benefits associated with each alternative must be measured. This task is obviously less than simple. However, a number of techniques for estimating the benefits of public programs have been developed. One technique employs the **willingness-to-pay criterion.** The value of a public concert sponsored by a city recreation department can be estimated by noting that people would pay $3, for instance, to attend the average concert. That price multiplied by the prospective number in attendance is some lower indication of the value or benefit of that recreational program. Similarly, the amount of money people spend to take advantage of a program is some indication that the patrons feel the program is worth at least what they spend. For instance, if a person takes off half a day of work and drives six miles to take a pet to a "free" rabies vaccination clinic, that program is worth at least the wages forgone plus the cost of going to and from the clinic. Of course, the willingness to pay for a program can be ascertained simply by surveying the target population and asking them how much, for example, they would be willing to pay for use of a traveling library bookmobile.

A second technique used to estimate the benefits accruing to programs involves the **savings criterion.** In this approach the amount of money saved by the program is the measure of the benefit. The Army Corps of Engineers uses this technique to estimate the benefit of building a dam to control flooding. The sum of insurance settlements and the value of lost crops from an average flood that would be saved by the dam is the benefit that would be attributable to the dam. The value of workers' sick leave time avoided by the enforcement of a safety helmet rule in the workplace similarly measures the benefit associated with a safety helmet program. The benefit of a smallpox vaccination program is partially measured by the number of lives that would be saved as a result of the inoculations. This saving is frequently put into dollar terms by estimating the lifetime wages that would be earned by each of the people "saved" by the vaccination.

A third technique commonly employed uses the **increase in capital value criterion.** Simply put, if a program makes the client or recipient more valuable, the increase in value measures the benefit of the program. For example, the value of a Ph.D. program in economics over bachelor's-level training would be the future earnings estimated for the average Ph.D. economist minus the projected earnings of the average person with a B.S. in economics. The benefit of developing a park would be measured by the increased property values of neighboring buildings.

While other techniques are available, most benefit attribution problems at the agency and program level can be attacked by variants of the techniques just sketched out. Needless to say, a number of techniques may be applied to the same project to tap a number of facets. A dam's benefits can be measured by the flood savings it provides, but the increase in the value of nearby land and the money people would spend to enjoy the recreation facilities also can be considered as measures of the program's benefits. A certain degree of ingenuity plus a bit of arbitrariness characterizes benefit attribution analysis. But, its advocates argue, these techniques allow the decision makers something more than seat-of-the-pants judgment in choosing among alternative programs to be included in a budget proposal.

The estimation of program costs can be more precise than the estimation of benefits. But many factors make costs hard to project. For one, budget requests at the federal level are prepared about a year before the fiscal year begins and projecting the costs of even common goods and services that far can be tricky, even if inflation is not involved. Often the state of the technology is unsettled and unforeseen difficulties mandate higher costs, as the sad experience of such military procurement debacles as the C-5A cargo plane witnesses.

An additional problem associated with estimating both costs and benefits relates to the time period over which the program or project will be useful. Benefits and costs over the lifetime of the project or program must be discounted to present value. The appropriate discount rate is often the subject of much discussion and disagreement, because the discount rate is crucial inasmuch as a small change in the discount rate used can often make what appears to be a desirable project less than cost effective.

Program budgets and the work involved in them are not usually visible in the budget document. Document 8 in the appendix reproduces a portion of a program budget and it is obvious that only the end results are displayed there. The best mix of alternative programs chosen are the ones in the budget document, along with some explanations of the programs. The real work characterizing the budget, the comparison of alternative programs, is not usually presented in justification materials that often accompany the budget to the oversight appropriations committees.

Just as successful implementation of the performance budget is not guaranteed by requiring work measures and cost accounting data to be included in the budget document, successful implementation of a program budget is not guaranteed by a program classification scheme, detailed narratives, or multi-year estimates. The budget must be *used* for program analysis and planning. Too often budget preparation is viewed as an obstacle course that agency personnel must run every year to satisfy the demands of the central budget office. If that attitude prevails, budgets will not be well utilized to evaluate or plan agency operations.

Agency personnel can be made to use new formats or collect and incorporate new data into the budget process and document, and so much of performance budgeting can be adopted at least in form. But in program budgeting new skills in addition to a favorable attitude are required. Knowledge of systems analysis and proficiency in cost effectiveness techniques are not widely distributed among agency personnel. Consequently, some resource obstacles are not easily overcome. Even where personnel with those skills are available, they often are not quickly or graciously admitted to the central decision-making centers in budget preparation. Moreover, program budgeting is expensive. The overall examination of programs required by the zero base budget concept multiplies the time required to prepare a budget. The Agriculture Department in the early 1960s attempted to build a budget that took nothing for granted and found that the effort was prodigious.[5] About one thousand persons spent thirty hours a week over a six-week period to prepare their budget, and the consensus was that the results were not appreciably different from what would have come from the traditional budget preparation process.

This discussion of budget types closes with a caution. In a sense "ideal types" have been presented. In the real world the budgets of few governmental units would neatly fit into one of these three types. The hybridization between object of expenditure and performance budgets also occurs among any and all the types that have been discussed. The type of budget, considered either as process or document, found in any jurisdiction is the result of political, administrative, and technical forces, each of which has a history of its own. Budgets, then, are unique to their setting. The description and discussion of budget types in this chapter, however, should allow the student of budgeting to understand the uniqueness of budgets wherever they are found.

BUDGET CHANGE AND POLITICS

The most successfully adopted budget innovation was the object of expenditure budget prepared under the aegis of the chief executive. This type of budget was and is practically universal. The performance budget is less widely adopted. If one assumes that a budget document incorporating activity classifications, narratives, workload data, and cost data signals adoption of a performance budget, according to Schick only seven of forty-eight states in the mid to late sixties had performance budgets. Only ten had three of the characteristics, six had two of the earmarks, ten claimed one characteristic, and fifteen possessed none of the four performance budget facets.[6]

Program budgeting has been less successfully adopted than performance budgeting. PPBS was required of all federal agencies by President Lyndon B. Johnson in 1965. By 1971 President Nixon's administration had backed away from the technique by no longer requiring that agencies submit program budgets.

At the state level a few adoptions were attempted and the results have not been overwhelming. While there was great variation on what states would call program budgets, a good number backed away from their infatuation with PPBS.

Why is it that budget innovations have not been successfully adopted more widely? There certainly is a need for efficient management of public organizations and no one can argue against planning and evaluation in the governmental sector. One set of obstacles has been suggested earlier in the description of the budget types. Most of those hindrances might be classified as bureaucratic, in the derogatory sense of the word. The unwillingness of agency personnel to develop meaningful work units, to learn the skills of the cost effectiveness analyst, to accept the system analyst into the decision-making circle, and the general unwillingness to change time-hallowed practices all militate against budget innovation. Additionally, lack of resources in the agencies reduces the likelihood of any kind of change. Most of these problems can be overcome with additional resources. People are willing to devote time to analysis and to accept new techniques and new workers if they are not threatened. When bureaucratic life is not perceived as a zero sum game, that is, one in which my gain is your loss, innovation is more easily accepted. The solution to a number of problems, then, lies in the availability of resources.

A second complex of factors that hinders budget innovation is external to the agencies. The budget document is the means by which executive requests are made to the legislature. Changes that would please the executive branch may not be viewed with favor in the legislature whose orientation, professionalization, and constituency differ from the agencies'. What a bureaucrat wants from a budget and what a legislator wants can be quite different. Changing the budget process or format will not necessarily change the use to which the budget is put and so may not have any real impact.

The less than determinative influence of a change in budget type on legislators is nicely demonstrated by James Jernberg's study of the impact of new kinds of budget information given to members of Congress.[7] In the early 1950s the federal budget document was changed by incorporating more performance budget type data. Information on workload and more managerially oriented matters was presented to appropriations committee personnel. The assumption behind much of budget reformers' activity is that changing the information input into the budget system would change the outputs or at least the behavior of those in the system. The expectation, therefore, was that when legislators were presented with the managerially relevant data, they would behave differently and would use the budget for more managerial oversight. In order to measure the effect of the new information, Jernberg did a content analysis of the kinds of questions posed by legislators to the agency personnel in the appropriations hearings. The results of the analysis indicated that in some subcommittees there was a change in the focus of questions after new information was introduced. In others, however, the orientation of the legislators was the same. A change in budget format does not necessarily change legislators' behavior. When there was an opportunity for different behavior, not all took advantage of it.

Wanat made a study that suggested the economizing orientation of oversight personnel would be evidenced in their behavior no matter what budget format they dealt with.[8] Over two hundred subjects were asked to assume the role of appropriations committee legislators. They were told of the legislators' desires to provide services, told to hold down spending, and presented with the "acceptable" ranges for budget cuts. These subjects then read the actual budget presentation made for the Department of Commerce's Office of Minority Business Enterprise for a recent year before the House Appropriations Committee. Although this presentation was couched in terms of the agency programs, half of the subjects were asked to "appropriate" money for the agency on a document in object of expenditure format and the other half worked with an activity classification format. The thinking of budget reformers would predict that the economizing orientation would be fostered by the object of expenditure format and hindered by the activity classification. More specifically, it was expected that the average cut made would be significantly larger by those using the object of expenditure format. Wanat found that there was no statistically significant difference. From this study one might infer that if legislator's orientations were economizing, they would cut irrespective of the kind of budget document they work with.

The fact that the executive branch uses a budget for one purpose or a set of purposes does not guarantee that the legislature will do the same, as the two studies cited indicate. Lack of support for an innovation from the funding body, the legislature, can sound the death knell.

A third set of hindrances to successful budget innovations relates to the need for or the applicability of the innovations. The world of governmental administration is not any more immune to the force of fads and fashions than the worlds of clothing and automobile styling. Faced with constant demands for services and provided with almost always inadequate resources, a proposal for change that promises solutions will certainly be viewed with some optimism. But what "worked" in the Department of Defense may not be applicable in the Labor Department. Or what worked at the federal level may not apply in Montana. Flushed with optimism over one successful adoption of a reform budget, reformers can unwittingly oversell the new idea. A program budget with its emphases on evaluation of alternatives would be better suited to analysis of new programs that are being considered for funding than for old and established programs well enmeshed in a web of clients, administrators, and legislators. Unfortunately, no one knows the limits of its applicability for any new technique. Consequently many innovations, budgetary and other varieties as well, are adopted and then either abandoned outright or kept in form but not in substance.

Successful budget innovation comes about because there is a need for it. The most widely adopted reforms — executive budgets and object of expenditure budgets — were successful because there was a crying need for accountability and those reforms were the only tools ready at hand that could meet the demands. The need for efficient operation, the need for planning, the need for program evaluation, and many other needs facing administrators are not solely "satisfiable" through the budget mechanism. Time-study teams often operate outside of the budget office, planning staffs have their own empires, and policy analysts are gaining recognition as legitimate professionals. Needs for some services consequently can be and are met outside the budget framework. Trying to satisfy all these needs through the budget can lead either to a charade in which the needs are met elsewhere or to an overloading of the budget mechanism because it cannot be all things to all people.

SUMMARY

Irrespective of type, all budgets have some common elements. Requests made by the agency are broken down into categories that are uniform across agencies, thus allowing comparability. Additionally, each agency or operating unit presents data for a period of years, which allows for comparability across time.

Three major budget types are identified and discussed. The object of expenditure budget categorizes agency requests according to the object for which money will be spent. Depending on the detail in this categorization, this type of budget allows both the legislator and the chief executive to exercise detailed control over agency operations.

The performance budget focuses attention on the activities the agency engages in so as to facilitate estimating the efficiency of the agency's operation. This type of budget, while still capable of being used for control purposes, is oriented to assisting in managing the organization.

The program budget, most recently seen in the form of a planning-programming-budgeting system (PPBS), is aimed at judging the effectiveness of program alternatives and in planning for the future. This approach utilizes quantitative techniques such as cost benefit analysis and systems analysis.

The adoption of various budget reforms is not a simple matter of administrative action. Problems encountered with the performance budget and more recently with the program budget were not only administrative, but also were problems involving political aspects of the organizations' environment. In particular, genuine budgetary reform has been hindered by resistance to change on the part of entrenched bureaucrats, by lack of resources, by the unwillingness of legislators to support change in the budget, and by the faddish nature of some budget "innovations" that did not really meet administrative needs.

NOTES

1. The discussion of budget types that follows draws heavily on two excellent pieces by Allen Schick: "The Road to PPB: The Stages of Budget Reform," *Public Administration Review* 26 (December 1966): 243–258 and *Budget Innovation in the States* (Washington, D.C.: The Brookings Institution, 1971).

2. William L. Riordon, *Plunkitt of Tammany Hall* (New York: E. P. Dutton and Co., Inc., 1963).

3. Schick, *Budget Innovation,* pp. 52–62.

4. The discussion of program budgeting in this chapter follows the presentation and organization found in Leonard Merewitz and Stephen H. Sosnick, *The Budget's New Clothes: A Critique of Planning-Programming-Budgeting and Benefit-Cost Analysis* (Chicago: Markham, 1971).

5. Arthur Hammond and Aaron Wildavsky, "Comprehensive Versus Incremental Budgeting in the Department of Agriculture," *Administrative Science Quarterly* 10 (December 1965): 321–346.

6. Schick, *Budget Innovation*, pp. 56–57.

7. James Jernberg, "Information Exchange and Congressional Behavior: A Caveat for PPB Reformers," *Journal of Politics* 33 (August 1969): 722–740.

8. John Wanat, "Budget Format and Budget Behavior," *Experimental Study of Politics* 2 (October 1973): 58–69.

SELECTED BIBLIOGRAPHY

Burkhead, Jesse. *Government Budgeting.* New York: Wiley, 1956.

Hammond, Arthur, and Wildavsky, Aaron. "Comprehensive Versus Incremental Budgeting in the Department of Agriculture." *Administrative Science Quarterly* 10 (December 1965): 321–346.

Harper, Edwin, Kramer, Fred A., and Rouse, Andrew M. "Implementation and the Use of PPB in Sixteen Federal Agencies." *Public Administration Review* 29 (November/December 1969): 623–632.

Havemann, Joel. *The Federal Budget: Reform's First Round.* Washington, D.C.: National Journal Reprints, n.d.

Horn, Stephen. *Unused Power: The Work of the Senate Committee on Appropriations.* Washington, D.C.: The Brookings Institution, 1970.

Howard, S. Kenneth. *Changing State Budgeting.* Lexington, Kentucky: Council of States Governments, 1973.

Jernberg, James. "Information Exchange and Congressional Behavior: A Caveat for PPB Reformers." *Journal of Politics* 33 (August 1969): 722–740.

Lee, Robert D., Jr., and Johnson, Ronald W. *Public Budgeting Systems.* Baltimore, Maryland: University Park Press, 1973.

Lyden, Fremont J., and Miller, Ernest G., eds. *Planning Programming Budgeting: A Systems Approach to Management,* 2nd ed. Chicago: Markham, 1971.

Merewitz, Leonard, and Sosnick, Stephen H. *The Budget's New Clothes: A Critique of Planning-Programming-Budgeting and Benefit-Cost Analysis.* Chicago: Markham, 1971.

Mosher, Frederick C., and Harr, John E. *Programming Systems and Foreign Affairs Leadership: An Attempted Innovation.* New York: Oxford University Press, 1970.

Nienaber, Jeanne, and Wildavsky, Aaron. *The Budgeting and Evaluation of Federal Recreation Programs, or Money Doesn't Grow on Trees.* New York: Basic Books, 1973.

Novick, David, ed. *Program Budgeting: Program Analysis and The Federal Budget.* Cambridge: Harvard University Press, 1965.

Prest, A. R., and Turvey, R. "Cost-Benefit Analysis: A Survey." *Economic Journal* 75 (December 1965): 683–735.

Riordon, William L. *Plunkitt of Tammany Hall.* New York: E.P. Dutton and Co., Inc., 1963.

Rivlin, Alice M. *Systematic Thinking for Social Action.* Washington, D.C.: The Brookings Institution, 1971.

Schick, Allen. *Budget Innovation in the States.* Washington, D.C.: The Brookings Institution, 1971.

———. "Control Patterns in State Budget Execution." *Public Administration Review* 24 (June 1964): 97–106.

———. "A Death in the Bureaucracy: The Demise of Federal PPB." *Public Administration Review* 33 (March/April 1973): 146–156.

———. "The Road to PPB: The Stages of Budget Reform." *Public Administration Review* 26 (December 1966): 243–258.

———. "Systems Politics and Systems Budgeting." *Public Administration Review* 29 (March/April 1969): 137–151.

Schultze, Charles L. *The Politics and Economics of Public Spending.* Washington, D.C.: The Brookings Institution, 1968.

Wanat, John. "Budget Format and Budget Behavior." *Experimental Study of Politics* 2 (October 1973): 58–69.

_____. "Bureaucratic Politics in the Budget Formulation Arena." *Administration and Society* 7 (August 1975): 191–212.

Wildavsky, Aaron. "The Political Economy of Efficiency: Cost-Benefit Analysis, Systems Analysis, and Program Budgeting." *Public Administration Review* 26 (December 1966): 292–310.

_____. "Political Implications of Budgetary Reform." *Public Administration Review* 21 (Autumn 1961): 183–190.

_____. "Rescuing Policy Analysis from PPBS." *Public Administration Review* 29 (March/April 1969): 189–202.

_____. *The Politics of the Budgetary Process,* 2nd ed. Boston: Little, Brown, 1974.

Chapter VI

BUDGETS AS RITUAL:

Incrementalism, Uncontrollability, and Expressive Action

The formulation and approval of a budget is an exercise in decision making. The process of budgeting can, in fact, be viewed as a sequence of decisions, each leading to another. Most observers and analysts of budgeting have characterized these budgetary decisions as incremental. It is the intent of this chapter to explore the notion of budgetary incrementalism first by describing incrementalism in general, then by examining its pervasiveness in budgeting, next by ascertaining the basis for it, and finally by explaining the functions it serves.

INCREMENTAL DECISION MAKING

Decisions are generally made by individuals or organizations when the status quo is threatened, disturbed, or judged somehow undesirable. For example, when one's automobile breaks down for the fifth time in as many months, a decision must be made about repairing or selling the vehicle. More germane to budgeting, when an agency's money is about to run out, the organization must decide whether to ask for more money and whether the request, if made, should be less, the same, or more than the previous year's amount. When an agency presents the appropriations committee with a budget request, that committee must decide how much to recommend to its parent chamber. The manner in which these and all decisions can be made varies considerably. Charles E. Lindblom has presented two polar types of decision making that are worth discussing.[1]

At one extreme of decision making is what Lindblom calls the **rational comprehensive** model. In this model the decision maker, faced with the need or at least the occasion for deciding an issue and being sure what must be sought or maximized, explores alternative ways of passing from the present undesired situation to the sought-for state. Having determined all possible or available alternative ways to the goal, the decision maker must utilize some criterion to identify the one alternative that would best attain the goal. As the name implies, this model is very comprehensive and also very rational. Unfortunately, it is not frequently used, even though it is advocated by and preached to governmental personnel.

As Lindblom points out, there are many problems involved in utilizing the rational comprehensive model of decision making. For one, even when the status quo is no longer desirable, it is usually not clear what the goal really is. Second, it is not possible to search out or examine all possible alternative means to a more satisfactory state of affairs. Not only are the resources for such a search not available, but even if all alternatives were known, unforeseen consequences of each alternative may make any choice a poor one. Additionally, choosing the appropriate criterion for selecting the "best" alternative cannot be easily done. For these reasons and many others the rational comprehensive model of decision making is not generally applicable and frequently cannot work. To get ahead of the story, in the budgetary arena the characteristics of PPBS and program budgeting in general are a manifestation of the rational comprehensive model. The relatively low incidence of program budgets underlines the difficulty of practicing rational and comprehensive decision making.

The model of decision making that characterizes how most decisions actually are made is what Lindblom calls **successive limited comparisons** or **disjointed incrementalism.** Incrementalism, as it shall be referred to in this chapter, differs from the rational comprehensive model on a number of dimensions. First, no attempt is made to optimize. Because the restrictions on resources are apparent, no one tries to investigate all possible solutions to the problem at hand to find the best alternative. Instead, alternatives are sequentially evaluated against a satisficing criterion. That is to say, a proposed solution is evaluated by asking if its likely results would be not optimal, but only satisfactory. Only if the alternative does not promise to be minimally acceptable does the search for a solution to the problem continue.

Secondly, the alternative solutions to the problem are not chosen out of the blue. The alternatives considered are only marginally or incrementally different from the unsatisfactory status quo. A timidity or conservatism is central to this approach. If the status quo is not satisfactory and some change is needed, the logic goes, it would be foolhardy to reject all that we know and are accustomed to in order to accept something that is alien. The known devil rather than the unknown devil will be chosen every day in this mode of thought. Because past experience and wisdom can be validly drawn upon only if slight deviations from the status quo are made, changes will inevitably be incrementally different from present practice, whence the name of this decision-making model.

A third crucial difference between the two polar decision-making models lies in the process used for selecting the alternative to the status quo. In the rational comprehensive scheme all alternatives are matched up with some agreed upon, impersonal, objective criterion. In the incremental model, however, it is recognized that decisions in collective groups, be they formal bureaucratic organizations, collegial legislative bodies, or atomistic mobs, are based on some degree of consensus among all the interested or affected parties. Because any change from the status quo in a collective body will affect many factions or segments of that body, unless some degree of concurrence develops regarding a proposed change, no matter how small, there is bound to be reluctance, hesitation, or even outright sabotage of the change. Incremental decisions, therefore, are basically political decisions, in the nonpartisan sense of political. Bargaining, gaming, and strategic notions therefore are commonly expected where incremental decision making is practiced.

Whenever incrementalism is being discussed two concepts must be elaborated: the status quo or **base** and the **increment** or marginal adjustment. Logically, to speak of incremental decision making there must first be some antecedent condition, the present, fixed, or stable point and second, a new condition or status that is only slightly different from the initial situation as a result of the decision. Thus, the base is the starting point and the increment is the change from that condition.

However, to be more than academic hair-splitting, the notion of incrementalism must be operationalized. That is to say, it must be possible to identify and somehow measure the status quo as well as the change from it. This requirement for operationalization is rather stringent and in general there have been relatively few solid and empirical studies of incremental decision making because of the inability to measure the decision-making base and the change. Was the decision to build a nuclear-powered aircraft carrier an incremental or a radical decision? If the status quo is taken as a weapons force that has had aircraft carriers, the decision may be viewed as incremental. On the other hand, if no nuclear-powered vessels of that size had ever been built, the decision would probably not be considered incremental.

Luckily, in budget matters it is relatively easy to measure the decision-making process and its results. Because of its cyclic nature, decisions are made at specific times and comparisons of the system a year apart will tell whether change has occurred. Because budgets are dollar expressions of programs, comparison of budgets at two time periods is easy. The appropriation, let us say, in year 1 is the base or status quo the agency is enjoying. The decision made by the agency personnel about what level of funding they desire finds expression in the dollar request they propose for the next year. If the difference is slight, the decision is said to be incremental. Similarly, comparison of the agency's request to what, to use the federal level as an example, the House

Appropriations Committee recommends allows determining if the committee's decision was incremental or not. The same kind of analysis can be applied to the decision of the House as applied to the recommendation of its committee, the Senate committee, the Senate as a whole, the conference committee's decision, and budget formulation decisions made earlier by the department and the central budget office.

In discussing incrementalism a crucial distinction must be made. Incrementalism can be used as a description of a decision-making process or as an explanation of a decision-making process. Explanatory incrementalism implies descriptive incrementalism, but descriptive incrementalism does not necessarily imply explanatory incrementalism. To understand that important statement, elaboration of both kinds of incrementalism is necessary.

DESCRIPTIVE INCREMENTALISM

It has generally been accepted in the last decade or two that most budgeting decisions are descriptively incremental. That is to say, in most jurisdictions, for most agencies, changes in appropriations from one year to the next have been small relative to the previous appropriations level. Within any given budget cycle there usually were only moderate changes in the original agency budget request as it goes from initiating agency, through the central budget office, and all the way to final legislative approval. The data presented in chapter 4 taken from the Labor Department budget formulation process showed that changes made by the department in the agencies' requests were relatively small compared to the requests. Likewise, budget bureau action on the department's recommendations was generally small. Data taken from Fenno also demonstrated the marginality of the changes made by congressional groups.

The descriptive incrementalism that occurs in the relations between the executive branch and the legislature can be succinctly expressed by statements (a) through (d)

$$\text{REQUEST}_t \geq \text{APPROPRIATIONS}_{t-1} \tag{a}$$
$$\text{APPROPRIATION}_t \geq \text{APPROPRIATION}_{t-1} \tag{b}$$
$$\text{APPROPRIATION}_t \leq \text{REQUEST}_t \tag{c}$$

The inequalities (a), (b), and (c) are
only marginally unequal (d)

In plain English, descriptive incrementalism says that agency requests in any year, t, are marginally greater than that agency's appropriation for the previous year. The appropriation in any year exceeds the previous year's appropriation by a small amount relative to the size of the appropriation. Lastly, the appropriation for an agency is somewhat less than what had been requested.

Recently there has been some evidence that the extent of budgetary incrementalism has been overestimated by earlier writers. Later in the chapter that question will be considered in some detail. No one, however, would question the assertion that descriptive incrementalism is generally prevalent. The important query is why incremental changes seem to prevail.

EXPLANATORY INCREMENTALISM

Incrementalism is proposed by some as an explanatory mechanism. That is to say, some scholars feel that the marginality of changes in budget figures (descriptive incrementalism) can be explained by some of the dynamics of decision making elaborated by Lindblom. The Lindblom reasoning would hold that lack of resources and the need for consensus puts a limit on what changes can be proposed or approved. While the explanatory incrementalism theory is plausible and attractive, there has been no systematic evidence collected to establish it firmly and unequivocably.

A series of studies by Davis, Dempster, and Wildavsky has attempted to show that strategic considerations on the part of budget process participants would generate budget results that comport with actual descriptively incremental budget results in the federal government.[2] For example, they demonstrate that congressional action on agency requests usually conforms to an equation like the following:

APPROPRIATION = b · (AGENCY REQUEST) + SLIGHT VARIATION

where b is a number less than but close to 1, such as .96. This can be interpreted as saying that Congress usually allows an agency 96 percent of its request. Davis, Dempster, and Wildavsky's research found that the "b"s in the equations for most agencies were, indeed, close to but less than 1. They infer that this is a result of strategic considerations on the part of a Congress that feels an agency's request is a good estimate of what the agency needs but is padded a bit and can therefore be cut down some.

The argument made by Davis, Dempster, and Wildavsky is based on the high proportion of the variance their models explain. It has been shown by Wanat, however, that the high correlations they find can be explained equally well by random variation within rather broad constraints that do not require any assumptions about the mechanics or mechanisms posited by Davis, Dempster, and Wildavsky.[3] This does not mean that the strategic explanation of incrementalism advanced by Davis, Dempster, and Wildavsky is erroneous; it does mean that their explanation has not been systematically established in their research.

To the extent that descriptive incrementalism occurs, then, how can it be explained? Why is it that relatively systematic evidence of descriptive incrementalism has been presented in much of the literature? An explanation is presented in this chapter that relies on the uncontrollability of governmental spending.

UNCONTROLLABILITY IN GOVERNMENT SPENDING

Because it is supposed to represent most closely the interests of the populace who provide money to run government, the legislative branch of government is generally considered to have the "power of the purse." The United States Constitution, in fact, says that "No money shall be drawn from the treasury but in consequence of appropriations made by law." Similar provisions hold in state and local governments. However, just because a legislative body is formally required to approve spending proposed by the executive does not mean that either one is really in control of the situation. In reality both the executive and the legislature often perform according to rules out of their control. Much of government spending is considered relatively uncontrollable.

Uncontrollability has two faces, one procedural and one substantive. **Procedural uncontrollability** refers to the situation in which no one person or institution is responsible for or able to control spending because of multiple channels of spending. **Substantive uncontrollability** refers here to the fact that whoever is formally in charge of spending is constrained by external forces to spend certain money on specific programs. Each of these will be considered in turn.

PROCEDURAL UNCONTROLLABILITY

Procedural uncontrollability is largely a result of organizational and jurisdictional fragmentation. In the federal government, for example, Congress has appropriations committees in each house. The expectation is that these two committees consider all bills that would have money drawn from the treasury. In reality they control money that will come out of the regular appropriations process explained in earlier chapters.

Unfortunately for control, there is the phenomenon of "backdoor spending."[4] This refers to the expenditure of money by legislative committees other than the appropriations committees. Each agency, it should be recalled, is supervised in each house by one committee that considers authorizing legislation and the appropriations committee, which considers money legislation. Legislation giving duties and powers to the Wage and Hour Division would be considered by the House Labor and Education Committee, but funding for implementing those duties would be considered by the House Appropriations Committee. Occasionally the "legislative" committee gets statutes enacted that allow the agency to expend money from the treasury without going to the appropriations committees or to go to those committees for a pro forma approval of decisions made elsewhere. Backdoor spending authority is usually found in three varieties: borrowing authority, contract authority, and permanent appropriations.

Borrowing or loan authority is given to an agency in enabling legislation. This means the agency is allowed to obligate and spend money from funds that are borrowed from the general public or from the treasury. In the federal government, borrowing authority was first given to the Reconstruction Finance Corporation in 1932 and has since been used many times. A more recent example is the authority to borrow money to back up student loan guarantees. While some might argue that this money is not really spent since it is only a loan and is paid back, it is important to note that both loans and expenditures take money from the treasury and so can have an influence on the impact of government spending on the economy. Occasionally these loans are forgiven and no repayment is made, which puts the "loans" in the category of being a straight expenditure. Apart from the considerations just noted, borrowing authority fragments the appropriations process in Congress because, until the 1974 reforms, no one committee coordinated or even monitored executive branch spending.

A second kind of backdoor spending is **contract authority.** Here an agency is given the power to enter into contracts for the purchase of goods or services. These contracts bind the government to paying off the obligations. The appropriations committees enter into the process in this kind of backdoor spending, but only as a rubber stamp since they know that the vendor who is a party to the contract has a legal right to payment. An example of this contract authority is the extension of low-rent public housing for FY1976; that authority increased contract commitments by $150 million. Needless to say, this kind of spending is uncontrollable in the short run.

A third kind of backdoor spending involves **permanent appropriations.** In this case the authorizing legislation specifies that the money must be paid, once again removing any discretion from the appropriations committees. A fixed amount of money is annually appropriated through permanent appropriations to each land grant college. The interest on the public debt is also covered through a permanent appropriation. Revenue sharing under the first authorization was also a permanent appropriation. While all these examples are permanent appropriations, the first was a fixed amount for an indefinite time, the second was of unspecified time and amount, and the last example was for a specified time and amount. In all of these instances the appropriations are uncontrollable by the committees theoretically responsible for controlling the expenditure of money.

The discussion thus far has focused on the inability of appropriations committees to control all spending. The executive branch is also constrained by forces outside of its control. The structures of permanent appropriations have to be respected by the executive branch as well as by the legislature. Yet executive branch personnel obviously enjoy some advantages in receiving money through backdoor spending. Contract and borrowing authority, for instance, free the agency from the restrictions of being tied to a rigid budget cycle and give it flexibility in the amount of money it manages. Permanent appropriations give the agency a certainty of funding not possible in the regular budget process.

SUBSTANTIVE UNCONTROLLABILITY

Substantive uncontrollability, on the other hand, binds both the legislature and the executive branch. Another and perhaps more descriptive term for substantive uncontrollability is **mandatory spending.** This spending often is passed through the regular appropriations committees, but those committees have no latitude in deciding how much to give. The agencies likewise have little or no leeway in deciding how much to ask for. Much of the mandatory spending is found in **entitlement programs** such as public assistance, veterans' pensions, black lung payments, and Medicare and Medicaid. In programs such as these the level of spending is determined by the number of eligible applicants. Every veteran entitled to a pension must receive it if the government is to retain the trust of its citizens. Therefore, spending is determined by factors outside the control of both the agency and the Congress. To be sure, there may be disagreement in the estimates of, for example, the number and amount of public assistance payments for the fiscal year under consideration. But to the degree that there is agreement on the estimates, the appropriations are uncontrollable.

The size of the uncontrollable portion of the federal budget is quite high. Table 6.1 breaks down the major components of the uncontrollables and makes it possible to see how little is left over after the mandatories are spelled out. Some research suggests that the proportion of the budget that is uncontrollable is increasing. John Gist, using a slightly different criterion for uncontrollability than that used in table 6.1, has presented data demonstrating that the uncontrollable portion of the budget has rather steadily risen from 40.1 percent in FY1965 to 71.1 percent in FY1977.[5] Gist's criterion is somewhat on the conservative side and the proportion probably is a bit higher.

Note that in table 6.1 the term "relatively uncontrollable" is used. It is possible for Congress to change the laws so that retirement pay for the military drops or to restrict eligibility for Social Security payments. Doing this, however, would not be politically likely and for that reason those categories are, in the short run at least, rather uncontrollable.

To this point controllability has referred to levels of spending set by the programs and their clients. Additional constraints are put on government spending at all levels by revenues. Most obviously, the estimated revenue for the fiscal year being considered, along with the size of an allowable deficit in the federal government, determines the overall spending level. J. Patrick Crecine speaks of "the great equation,"[6] which for our purposes can be expressed as follows:

BUDGET SIZE= ESTIMATED REVENUE + ACCEPTABLE DEFICIT

For state and local governments, which generally cannot plan an operating budget deficit, the revenue estimated puts a strong limit on what the executive can propose and what the legislature can allow.

To complicate matters further, not all revenues are available for spending in all programs. Money taken in that is not earmarked for specific purposes goes into a **general fund** that the chief executive can propose spending anywhere. But governments often have **trust funds** that earmark all money collected

TABLE 6.1. CONTROLLABILITY OF BUDGET OUTLAYS (IN BILLIONS OF DOLLARS).

	FY1967 (ACTUAL)	FY1974 (ESTIMATE)
Relatively uncontrollable:		
Under present law:		
Social insurance trust funds	30.3	80.4
Interest on the debt	12.5	24.7
Veterans benefits	4.9	9.1
Public assistance (including Medicaid)	4.2	14.8
Farm price supports (CCC)	1.7	2.7
Military retired pay	1.8	4.7
Postal operations	.8	1.4
Legislative and judiciary	.3	.8
Other	2.4	8.0
Revenue sharing	—	6.0
Subtotal	58.9	152.6
Allowance for pay raises	—	3.7
Outlays from prior year obligation and contract authority	41.3[a]	45.5
Total relatively uncontrollable	100.2	201.8
Relatively controllable:		
National defense	44.6[a]	52.3
Civilian programs	17.6	23.7
Total relatively controllable	62.2	76.0

SOURCE: U.S., Congress, Joint Study Committee on Budget Control, "Improving Congressional Control Over Budgeting Outlay and Receipt Totals," 93d Congress, 1st Session, House Report No. 93–13, 1973, Washington, D.C.: U.S. Government Printing Office, p. 22.
a. Partially estimated.

from, say, the state lottery for spending on education. Or the highway system gets all the money collected from taxes on gasoline. Or the money taken out of wages for old-age assistance can only be used for that purpose. In a similar vein are **public enterprise** or **revolving funds** frequently associated with government corporations; all money taken in by the government enterprise is plowed back into the operations of that corporation. Both the chief executive and the legislature find themselves in strained circumstances because of earmarking. For instance, there may be a surplus of money in a state trust fund for spending on highways, but the real transportation problem lies in the need for mass transit in urban areas. Money, however, can typically neither be requested nor allowed from the trust fund for urban mass transit.

Controllability of the budget is further reduced when the notion of "base" or status quo is brought into play. There is ample evidence that the previous appropriation is generally considered to be the base or given figure upon which all budget calculations and decisions are made. The base is considered to be a given figure by both the agencies and the Congress. One writer emphasizes this point by noting:

> For instance, the budget justification materials given Congress by the agencies routinely and regularly spelled out the increases requested over last year's base and the purposes to which the increases were to be put. Questioning in the hearings focused on the requested increases. The prose portion of Congressional appropriations reports almost always dealt entirely with the reasons for allowing or disallowing the increment requested and seldom paid any attention to the total amount requested. . . . All of this points to the fact that Congress specifically focuses on the increments and not on the total amount requested.[7]

After making the distinction between the base and the increment, Crecine's equation is now expressable as follows:

PREVIOUS APPROPRIATION + INCREASES =
ESTIMATED REVENUE + ACCEPTABLE DEFICIT

The estimated revenue for a given year will not be much different from the revenue of the previous year since the revenue base depends on population, economic productivity, and other nongovernable elements that are usually slow changing in the short run. The size of a deficit is also hemmed in by political realities. This means that any changes in the righthand side of the equation will be slow and marginal. Since the right side of this equation is largely fixed by forces outside the control of budget process participants and since the previous appropriation is rarely touched, all the "action" in the budget process centers on the increases over the previous appropriation.

Budget increases are divisible into two broad classes, the programmatic increases and the mandatory increases. Entitlement programs that are growing will constitute some of the increase. The simple cost of delivering the same services as last year will also eat up some of the possible increases because of the inflated costs of purchasing the same goods as last year. Some of the increase will be in expansion of old programs. Needless to say, it is only in the programmatic area that discretion is really possible.

The mandated increases in budgets alone allow explanation of the incrementalism that has characterized much of budgetary phenomenon and that was expressed earlier in statements (a) through (d). What typically happens is that the agency's request is somewhat larger than it was in the previous year because some increase is mandated by such forces as wage increases, inflation, and growth of entitlements and also because the agency seeks to expand or enrich its programs. Thus, it is obvious why an agency's request for a given year exceeds its previous year's appropriation. The legislature is aware of the mandatory nature of some of the agencies' requests and knows that those increases must be honored if faith is to be kept with the clientele of the agency. At the same time the legislature knows that it can cut the requests for the new programs, and it usually does that to some degree. Consequently, because it allows the mandatory requests to pass practically untouched, each year's appropriation usually surpasses its predecessor. But since the programmatic portion of the increase is usually reduced, the appropriation is less than the request. Finally, because the mandated increases were caused by demographic changes or economic changes, both of which are generally marginal from one year to the next, and because revenue changes are not radical from one year to the next, all of the inequalities express slight or incremental change.

THE EXTENT OF INCREMENTALISM

It has been possible, by utilizing the distinction between controllable and uncontrollable spending, to account for the descriptive incrementalism that has been observed by so many analysts of budget phenomena. This is not to say that the strategy or bargaining interpretation of budgetary decision making does not apply. If it does apply, it can only be a good explanation on that part of the budget request where there is discretion, the programmatic or controllable requests. Gist has shown that incrementalism does not pervade the more controllable budgets.[8] Incrementalism, therefore, is not universal in its explanatory form. There are indications, moreover, that descriptive incrementalism is not as universal as was once thought.[9]

To this point incrementalism has been discussed as though it were a unitary concept, one whose characteristics were agreed upon. Words like "slight," "marginal," and "small" have been used to describe the changes in appropriations and requests. One analyst's interpretation of "small" could appear to be "moderate" to another analyst. Consequently, some discussion is needed to define terms so as to specify where descriptive incrementalism occurs and where it does not. This section presents recent reseach that underlines the variability of the notion and the applicability of incrementalism.

The point that incrementalism is not a clear and discrete concept has been nicely demonstrated by Jon Bond and Peter Bock in a study of budgeting in United Nations agencies.[10] They examined expenditures in the Regular Budget, the Specialized Agencies, Voluntary Programs, and Peacekeeping Operations in the period 1946 through 1972. The Regular Budget and the Specialized Agencies expenditures manifested stable incremental growth, while expenditures on Peacekeeping Operations were neither stable nor incremental.

Bond and Bock suggest that the degree of incrementalism characterizing the budget process reflects the degree of consensus about the legitimacy of the activities. Their work suggests that incrementalism would probably be more prevalent in older agencies that are well established in a constellation of ties to legislators, clients, and other supporters who either have a claim on the agency or in some way are stably connected to it and thereby legitimize it. New agencies would probably not have incremental appropriations patterns.

All the research done on budgetary behavior until rather recently has been at the agency level. The unit of analysis was invariably the entire agency's budget. Peter Natchez and Irvin Bupp argue that if one moves from the agency level down to the program level, incrementalism tends to disappear.[11] Their analysis of the Atomic Energy Commission demonstrated that in the formulation of the agency's budget there was very strong variation in the amounts proposed for the programs. In no way could the adjective incremental characterize the program-level changes. If, however, one examined the change in the entire agency's budget, incrementalism did seem to describe the change. Fluctuations at the program level, it appears, tend to cancel each other out when aggregated, thus giving the appearance of stable and moderate change.

The dependence of incrementalism on the mode of measurement suggested by Natchez and Bupp's work finds corroboration in some research by Wanat.[12] Incrementalism is thought to be regularized, routinized, and predictable. This has been shown by the high correlations between agency requests and legislature's approval. The legislature, it is argued, takes cues from the agencies to reduce its rationality costs and so the regular association is observed. Wanat analyzed the correlations between agency requests and legislative appropriations for a dozen agencies in the 1950s and 1960s. The correlation between the requests and appropriations were uniformly high. He also examined the requests, not for dollars, but for personnel and what Congress allowed of those requests. The correlations between personnel requested and personnel allowed for the same agencies were generally lower than the comparable correlations on the dollar data. This difference suggests that measuring budgetary interaction with data that is not subject to inflation leads to the conclusion that Congress is not as easily led by the agencies as once thought. If Congress is acting more independently, the regularity and routinization of the interaction associated with incrementalism no longer holds as strongly and incrementalism may not apply as much as thought.

One last piece of research casts more doubt on the incremental model of budgetary decision making. Central to the notion of incrementalism is the inviolability of the status quo or the base. What has been decided in the past, that is, the size of the last appropriation, is taken as a given figure and attention is focused on the deviations from that base figure. John Gist has suggested that at the national level this inviolability of the base no longer holds.[13] He notes that from FY1965 to FY1977 the increase in the uncontrollables exceeded the total increase in the budget half the time. The only way this could happen is if the base were cut into. Gist argues that incursions are made into the base as a result of increasing uncontrollables and so the distinction central to incremental decision making is no longer valid. Incrementalism therefore must be reconsidered or the limits of its applicability clearly defined.

In all fairness it must be admitted that although incrementalism is under attack as an explanatory tool, as a description of most budgetary behavior it still holds a fair degree of power.

BUDGETS AS EXPRESSIVE ACTION

In this chapter budgets have been presented as being largely out of the control of both the executive and the legislature. Priority setting and policy making in the budget process consequently take place in that portion of the budget that is not "spoken for" by decisions made years ago. Budget participants are aware of the controllable/uncontrollable distinction spelled out, and they prepare and pass budgets containing both kinds of money. The question considered in this last section is why so much time and effort are expended on matters over which there is so little control.

For the executive branch the question is rather easily answered. Even if all veterans applying for pensions must receive them, there is still the problem of estimating how many new applicants for pensions will be eligible in the fiscal year being considered. Mundane problems of going through the motions of determining the size of the uncontrollable portion of the budget require the involvement of the executive branch personnel. But why would legislature personnel go through the time and trouble to review matters beyond their control?

Consider the nature of legislative involvement in budget approval. That process has been characterized as regular, routinized, systematic, predictable, even repetitious. The same people engage in the same kind of behavior year after year. Almost everyone knows everyone else on sight. The same concerns are expressed in almost every hearing. The same justifications and defenses are preferred each year. The same admonitions are advanced. To be sure, there is variety from year to year, but such variation is variation on a theme.

Weidenbaum describes congressional budget activity with regard to some of the mandatory items in the following fashion: "The law requires monthly payments to all those certified by VA doctors as possessing a given percentage impairment of earnings. However, in this case the Congress insists on annually reviewing the appropriation for the payment of veterans' pensions and compensation. It is hard to characterize the congressional review as anything other than wheel spinning or having 'fun and games' with the budget."[14] Such behavior is reminiscent of the corollary of Parkinson's Law relating to budget decision making wherein all time and attention is devoted to a very minor expenditure while major decisions are made in a twinkling of the eye. Similarly, Ira Sharkansky's analysis of budget relations at the state level gave evidence of the legislatures following the governors' leads in most cases. If this is the way things tend to go, it is evident that at least some of budgetary decision making is not instrumental.

If not instrumental, budgeting to some degree must serve expressive ends. A very tantalizing suggestion has been made by Johan P. Olsen in his study of budgeting in a Norwegian commune.[15] He finds that little instrumental decision making takes place in the budgeting arena. Yet there is a good amount of participation. Olsen interprets the Norwegian situation to be one in which budgeting is a ritual and therefore not instrumental but expressive in purpose. Given the relatively uncontrollable nature of budgeting, it is very possible that budgeting in general, and particularly for those involved in approving budgets, is ritual behavior and consequently is primarily expressive.

If Olsen is correct, the participation of legislators in examining the largely uncontrollable budgets is explicable. Ritual activity is usually stylized, repetitive, routinized, and predictable, all of which apply to budgeting. Ritual, Olsen says, serves two general functions: to legitimate and to satisfy cognitive and affective needs of "followers."[16] In approval of budgets, be the content wholly mandated or not, legislators are able to legitimize themselves by going through motions that will impress their constituents and casual observers with their involvement and diligence. The citizen wants and needs to know that someone is in charge or that someone is overseeing those in charge. The ritual of budgeting tells the citizen that at least some legislators are doing what is expected and thereby enhances the legitimacy of the legislature.

In the American state context Anton has come to conclusions similar to Olsen's. The participants in state budgeting engage in heavily symbolic action according to Anton because much of what they do is out of their control. This applies to agency personnel, the governor, and the legislature. "What is at stake in the performance of the roles . . . is not so much the distribution of resources, about which state actors have little to say, but the distribution of symbolic satisfaction among the involved actors and the audiences which observe their stylized behavior."[17]

These suggestions of the ritual nature of budgeting are not meant to imply that actual instrumental decisions are not made. After all, not all of the budget is uncontrollable. While expressive forces undeniably have some impact on decisions in the controllable portion of the budget, other forces also have some influence. In the next chapter some of those forces are examined in an attempt to understand the politics in budgets.

SUMMARY

Decision making in the budget process is generally thought to be incremental. That is, decisions made in the formulation and approval phases typically have results that are only marginally different from the status quo. This descriptive kind of incrementalism has been moderately well established. Some budget scholars also feel that marginal departures from the status quo can also be explained by notions of strategy, gaming, and resource deficiencies. Problems with those explanations are discussed and an alternative explanation based on budget uncontrollability is preferred.

Budgets can be both procedurally and substantively uncontrollable. Procedural uncontrollability is a result of organizational and jurisdictional fragmentation reflected in backdoor spending practices such as loan authority, contract authority, and permanent appropriations. Substantive uncontrollability refers to spending that is mandated in some fashion by law, such as entitlement programs, earmarked revenue sources, and inflationary forces. Because legislatures will usually honor mandated requests but not all of the nonmandated requests and because revenue constraints and uncontrollables allow a slight increase in the requests, the descriptive incrementalism commonly observed is explicable. However, evidence exists that the incrementalism thought to be prevalent in domestic agencies does not always exist at the program level or in the nondomestic arena.

Because of the uncontrollability of so much of the budget, it is suggested that some of budgeting really serves ritual, symbolic, and expressive rather than instrumental ends.

NOTES

1. Charles E. Lindblom, "The Science of 'Muddling Through,'" *Public Administration Review* 29 (Spring 1959): 79–88.

2. Otto A. Davis, M. A. H. Dempster, and Aaron Wildavsky, "A Theory of the Budgetary Process," *American Political Science Review* 60 (September 1966): 529–547; "On the Process of Budgeting II: An Empirical Study of Congressional Appropriations," in *Studies in Budgeting,* R. F. Byrne, A. Charnes, W. W. Cooper, O. A. Davis, and Dorothy Gilford, eds. (New York: North Holland Publishers, 1971); "Toward a Predictive Theory of Government Expenditures: U.S. Domestic Appropriation," *British Journal of Political Science* 4 (October 1974): 419–452.

3. John Wanat, "Bases of Budgetary Incrementalism," *American Political Science Review* 68 (September 1974): 1221–1228.

4. See the discussion in Joint Study Committee on Budget Control, "Recommendations for Improving Congressional Control Over Budgetary Outlay and Receipt Totals," House Report No. 147, 93d Congress, 1st Session, 1973 (Washington D.C.: Government Printing Office, 1973), pp. 10–12.

5. John R. Gist, " 'Increment' and 'Base' in the Congressional Appropriations Process," paper presented at the annual meeting of the Midwest Political Science Association, 1976, Chicago, table 1.

6. John P. Crecine, "Defense Budgeting: Organizational Adaptation to External Constraints," Memorandum RM-6121-PR (Santa Monica, California: The RAND Corporation, March 1970), p. 13.

7. Wanat, p. 1225.

8. John R. Gist, *Mandatory Expenditures and the Defense Sector* (Beverly Hills, California: SAGE Publications, 1974).

9. See, for example, Randall B. Ripley and Grace A. Franklin, eds., *Policy-Making in the Federal Executive Branch* (New York: Free Press, 1975).

10. Jon R. Bond and P. G. Bock, "Budgetary Incrementalism in the United Nations: An Empirical Investigation," mimeo, University of Illinois-Urbana, July 1975.

11. Peter B. Natchez and Irvin C. Bupp, "Policy and Priority in the Budgetary Process," *American Political Science Review* 67 (September 1973): 951–963.

12. John Wanat, "Personnel Measures of Budgetary Interaction," *Western Political Quarterly* 29 (June 1976): 295–297.

13. Gist, " 'Increment' and 'Base.' "

14. Murray L. Weidenbaum, "Institutional Obstacles to Reallocating Government Expenditures," in Robert H. Haveman and Julius Margolis, eds., *Public Expenditures and Policy Analysis* (Chicago: Markham, 1970), p. 243.

15. Johan P. Olsen, "Local Budgeting, Decision-Making or a Ritual Act?" *Scandinavian Political Studies* 5 (1970): pp. 85–118.

16. Ibid., p. 103.

17. Thomas J. Anton, "Roles and Symbols in the Determination of State Expenditures," *Midwest Journal of Political Science* 11 (1967): 39.

SELECTED BIBLIOGRAPHY

Anton, Thomas J. *The Politics of State Expenditure in Illinois.* Urbana: University of Illinois Press, 1966.

————. "Roles and Symbols in the Determination of State Expenditures." *Midwest Journal of Political Science* 11 (1967): 27–43.

Bond, Jon R., and Bock, P. G. "Budgetary Incrementalism in the United Nations: An Empirical Investigation." Mimeo, University of Illinois-Urbana, July 1975.

Caiden, Naomi, and Wildavsky, Aaron. *Planning and Budgeting In Poor Countries.* New York: Wiley, 1974.

Crecine, John P. *Defense Budgeting: Organizational Adaptation to External Constraints.* Santa Monica, California: The RAND Corporation, Memorandum RM-6121-PR, March 1970.

————. *Governmental Problem Solving.* Chicago: Rand McNally, 1969.

Danziger, James N. "Assessing Incrementalism in British Municipal Budgeting." *British Journal of Political Science* 6 (1976): 335–350.

Davis, Otto A.; Dempster, M. A. H.; and Wildavsky, Aaron. "On the Process of Budgeting II: An Empirical Study of Congressional Appropriations." In *Studies in Budgeting,* edited by R. F. Byrne, A. Charnes, W. W. Cooper, O. A. Davis, and Dorothy Gilford. New York: North Holland Publishers, 1971.

————. "A Theory of the Budgetary Process." *American Political Science Review* 60 (September 1966): 529–547.

————. "Towards A Predictive Theory of Government Expenditures: U.S. Domestic Appropriations." *British Journal of Political Science* 4 (October 1974): 419–452.

Derthick, Martha. *Uncontrollable Spending for Social Services.* Washington, D.C.: The Brookings Institution, 1975.

Gist, John R. "The Effect of Budget Controllability on the Theory of Incrementalism." Paper presented at the annual meeting of the Midwest Political Science Association, Chicago, April 1974.

_____. " 'Increment' and 'Base' in the Congressional Appropriations Process." *American Journal of Political Science* 21 (May 1977): 341–352.

_____. *Mandatory Expenditures and the Defense Sector.* SAGE American Politics Series, Number 04–049. Beverly Hills, California: SAGE Publications, 1974.

Hoole, Frank W.; Job, Brian L.; and Tucker, Harvey J. "Incremental Budgeting and International Organizations." *American Journal of Political Science* 20 (May 1976): 273–301.

Kim, Sun Kil. "The Politics of a Congressional Budgetary Process: 'Backdoor Spending.' " *Western Political Quarterly* 21 (December 1968): 606–623.

Lindblom, Charles E. "The Science of 'Muddling Through.' " *Public Administration Review* 19 (1959): 79–88.

Natchez, Peter B., and Bupp, Irvin C. "Policy and Priority in the Budgetary Process." *American Political Science Review* 67 (September 1973: 951–963.

Olsen, Johan P. "Local Budgeting, Decision-Making or a Ritual Act?" *Scandinavian Political Studies* 5 (1970): 85–118.

Ripley, Randall B., and Franklin, Grace A., eds. *Policy-Making in the Federal Executive Branch.* New York: Free Press, 1975.

Sharkansky, Ira. "Agency Requests, Gubernatorial Support, and Budget Success in State Legislatures." *American Political Science Review* 62 (December 1968): 1220–1231.

U.S. Congress, House, Joint Study Committee on Budget Control. "Recommendation for Improving Congressional Control Over Budgetary Outlay and Receipt Totals." 93d Congress, 1st Session, House Report No. 93–147. Washington, D.C.: Government Printing Office, 1973.

Wanat, John. "Bases of Budgetary Incrementalism." *American Political Science Review* 68 (September 1974): 1221–1228.

_____. "Personnel Measures of Budgetary Interaction." *Western Political Quarterly* 29 (June 1976): 295–297.

Weidenbaum, Murray L. "Institutional Obstacles to Reallocating Government Expenditures." In *Public Expenditures and Policy Analysis,* edited by Robert H. Haveman and Julius Margolis. Chicago: Markham, 1970.

———. "On the Effectiveness of Congressional Control of the Public Purse." *National Tax Journal* 18 (December 1965): 370–374.

Wildavsky, Aaron. "The Annual Expenditure Increment — or How Can Congress Regain Control of the Budget?" *The Public Interest* 33 (Fall 1973): 84–108.

Chapter VII

BUDGETS AS POLITICS:

Influences

On Budget Decisions

P olitics has been defined by Harold Lasswell as "who gets what, when, and how." A moment's reflection on that definition makes it clear that budgeting is part and parcel of politics. The "what" is money, be it expressed in requests, appropriations, or expenditures. The "who" are the various actors described in chapter 4 along with the ultimate recipients of government spending. The "when" was presented in the chronology of chapter 3. The "how" (and the "why") is the focus of this chapter.

The "how" of budget allocations is a complex and largely unexplored territory. The vast number of governments and the even wider range of programs they undertake suggest that no one explanation of "how" money is allocated would universally apply. The variation introduced into the budget process by the individual differences of the participants further complicates understanding "how" money is allocated. When the press of idiosyncratic events is added to the budget process, "how" resources are distributed becomes even harder to comprehend. These problems, however, do not imply that the politics of budgeting is beyond analysis.

Indeed, recent research has uncovered a great deal of data on the behavior of those involved in budgeting. This research largely follows a behavioral mode of inquiry, which puts some of it into a quantitative research style. In this chapter a representative sampling of that research is presented, but especially for the sake of those without much quantitative research background, the research is presented in an easily understandable manner.

Just how is politics to be measured in the budgetary arena? In this chapter the "who" is at times the agency, the department, the central budget office, the chief executive, the appropriations committees and their subcommittees, as well as the legislative chambers as a whole. Since decision making in budgeting is largely sequential, the question asked is how does each of these actors get what he or she wants or how do they make their authoritative decisions. The measurement of their actions, the dependent variable, will depend on the research being reviewed. It may be the raw dollar amount requested or appropriated; it may be the percentage increase over the previous year; it may be the percentage of what was sought; it may be the raw increase over what was appropriated or the raw decrease of what was requested. In all cases, who wins and who loses will be measured by how well they achieved their monetary goals.

If the stakes for which the participants are playing and their measurement are relatively well settled, the explanation of how and why one wins or loses is not. Many explanations have been advanced about how and why money is appropriated. The remainder of this chapter presents explanations of some theories of how and why budget decisions are made.

Two relatively broad theories of budget decision making have already been presented. In chapter 4 the roles of budget participants were advanced to make understandable much of the budget behavior. And in chapter 6 the impact of constraint on budget behavior was considered. In this chapter those two theories or approaches to understanding budget politics are presented, followed by explanations based on partisanship, substance of the budget, strategy, and demand. Role and constraint explanations are presented once again because they form the ground rules under which the other forces operate. They are similar to the notion of party identification in voting behavior. The partisan affiliation of a voter is the basic predisposition pressing on the voter. Issues and candidates only serve to modify that basic predisposition. So too in budget phenomena. The roles of the participants along with the constraints they must work under set the major direction of their decisions. The personalities, demands, ideology, substance, strategies, partisanship, and many other forces work to modify the influence of the roles and constraints.

INSTITUTIONAL ROLE AND CONSTRAINT EXPLANATIONS OF BUDGET POLITICS

Budget formulation and approval involves a relatively small set of participants who act in somewhat predictable ways. The predictability is a result of the repeated interaction with each other, which leads to mutual expectations of how each actor should and generally does behave. The agency personnel seek to expand their budget while the department-level officials try to balance the programmatic drives of the agencies with the fiscal concerns of those higher up in the executive branch; consequently, they usually reduce agency requests. Central budget officials and the chief executive seek further to reduce departmental recommendations for expansion because they are given the mission of presenting a fiscally prudent budget and because they feel that the operative agents in the executive branch are overly expansive. The legislators, it will be remembered, also tend to cut requests coming from the executive branch. This is a consequence of the legislators' being expected by their constituents to wield a paring knife on the executive budget as well as their experience that such paring has in the past not crippled the bureaucratic apparatus.

It should be noted that since variations exist in agencies' growth rates and legislative treatment of agencies' requests, the role explanation is not fully satisfactory.

The patterns of budget behavior elaborated in chapter 4 and summarized above do not directly address the question of "who gets what." Since the desires of the executive and legislative branches are generally opposed, the question is still who wins or, more accurately, who wins more or more often. It is important to sound the cautionary note that asking whether the executive branch or the legislative branch is more powerful in the budget process is an oversimplified and misleading question inasmuch as no one answer can be given. However, there are some data that can at least illuminate the interplay between the two major governmental institutions.

Ira Sharkansky's study of the budgetary relations between the governor, the agencies, and the legislatures in nineteen states in the mid-1960s provides an enlightening picture of the budgetary power of the governor in most states.[1] In the states Sharkansky examined the legislature is provided in the budget document not only with the appropriations recommended by the governor but also the amount originally requested by the agencies. Sharkansky asked whether the legislators looked to the governor for cues on what to appropriate, whether they looked to the agencies, or whether they were influenced by both the agency requests and the gubernatorial recommendations. By means of causal analysis it was inferred that in most cases the line of greatest influence on the legislature came directly from the governor. The governor's recommendation had in turn been influenced by the agencies' requests. In a good number of cases the legislatures' decisions were jointly influenced by the agencies' requests and the governors' recommendations. The crucial point to notice is that almost without exception legislators' decisions were heavily influenced by the chief executive's decisions.

Much of what Sharkansky found is explicable because of the modest resources available to the legislators and what might be called an occupational bias. State legislators are typically part-time workers. Few states pay their legislators enough money to support themselves and their families. Coupled with the fact that few legislatures meet year-round, most legislators simply do not have the time to delve deeply into agency operations and budget requests to make fully independent decisions in appropriations matters. Additionally, most legislators, no matter what the level of government, lack staff resources that would theoretically enable them to make independent decisions. Given those resource constraints, legislators must look outside themselves for guidance on appropriations decisions.

The advice legislators get from the bureaucrats is usually viewed with some hesitance. The agency recommendation on spending can hardly be viewed as coming from an unbiased and disinterested party. But governors' recommendations would meet a more receptive audience. For one, they know more of "the big picture" regarding the balance of revenues and expenditures than do individual agencies. Second, unlike the bureaucrat, governors are to be trusted because they are politicians and so are similar to the legislators. The politician, unlike the bureaucrat, can be expected to be realistic, responsible, and understanding of the legislators. Since governors are like them, legislators will more easily accept their advice.

Whether it is the chief executive or the individual agencies that influence the decisions made by the legislators, it is important to note that it is executive branch personnel who are considered to be the "influencers." No matter what budget arena one examines, it is almost certain that there will be a very high correlation between the request made by the executive branch and the appropriation from the legislative branch. In numerous studies the results have shown a statistically significant correlation between the request and the appropriation, irrespective of whether the operationalizations are raw total dollars, increments measured in raw dollars, or various percentage measures. The same results occur whether the data analyzed are across agencies at one point in time, across agency averages, or over time. Especially since the agency request precedes the appropriation, these results would imply that the executive branch dominates the legislature in budgeting. Such an interpretation would be partially justified on the grounds of institutional role but would be partially misleading because of composition and measurement problems.

Institutionally, the executive branch must initiate the budget process. Legislators have neither the skill nor the desire to put together documents embodying the needs and desires of agencies. In fact, the establishment of the executive budget signals legislative abdication of the practice of initiating the budget process. Because agencies operate under a statutory charter endorsed by the legislature, they in theory are merely acting out the will of the legislature. In reality, because of the agency's expertise, the legislature comes to rely on the expertise and so the power of the agency. Therefore if an agency asks for a lot of money, it is reasonable to assume it will get a goodly amount. If it asks for a smaller amount, its lead will be taken and a small amount is likely to be given.

While the statistical relationship between executive branch requests and appropriations is high and while there is good reason for the legislative over-seers to follow the lead of the executive branch, it would be inaccurate to infer that the executive branch dominates the budget process. As the last chapter indicated, much of what the executive branch requests is mandated and out of the control of any governmental actor — at least in the short run. One cannot infer that a legislature is subservient to the executive in appropriating the amounts requested by the executive if the executive is forced by laws (passed by the legislature, it is well to remember) to ask for those amounts. A high correlation between the request and the appropriation is to be expected because of the composition of the request.

The manner in which the size of the agency request and legislature appropriation is measured further leads to an inaccurate assessment of the budgetary relations between the two branches. Almost invariably when quantitative analyses of legislative-executive relationships are undertaken, the operationalization of agency desires is taken to be the raw budget request, the increase over what the agency had last year, or a percentage increase over what the agency was last appropriated. In all of these cases the basic unit of analysis is the dollar. Because of inflation, to mention but one complication, the dollar request may not be a good measure of what an agency really wants. To keep up with increasing costs as well as mandated duties, the amount of money needed to finance the same activities grows. New programs and enhancement of old programs also are expressed in dollars and there is no very easy way to disentangle requests for mandated costs from requests for expansion. It is reasonable to expect, and there is evidence to back up the expectation, that legislatures agree to requests for mandated increases but do not necessarily do the same for programmatic increases.[2] Since most of the budget is mandated in one sense or another, one would expect to find a high correlation between executive branch requests and legislative appropriations.

One attempt to disentangle the mandated from the programmatic elements of agency requests in order to clarify the relationship between the legislative and executive branch used both personnel and money measures of budget requests.[3] Working on the assumption that a requested increase in dollars over the previous year's appropriation would have both inflated and mandated components but a requested increase in the number of persons would not have any "inflation" component, Wanat analyzed the correlations among increases requested by the executive branch, the cut in the requested increase made by Congress, and the consequent growth over the previous appropriation based on both dollar and personnel data. The correlations between the request and the appropriation on the dollar data for twelve federal agencies in the 1950s and 1960s were, as would be expected, quite high. This would lead to the conclusion that Congress "followed" the executive branch recommendations embodied in the requests. However, when the correlations between the same two variables were computed on the personnel data, the correlations, while still high, were substantially lower than those on the dollar data. On the more programmatic measure of budgetary interaction between the two branches, Congress appears not to follow the lead suggested by the executive. One cannot take for granted, therefore, that the executive branch dominates the legislature.

In the same study the correlations between legislative action on the request (the cut) and the change from the previous appropriation (the growth) were computed. A negative correlation would suggest that the greater the cut, the more the growth would be reduced. The relationship was very weak on the dollar data. The relationship was strengthened using the personnel data. That is to say, changes made by Congress in the more programmatic personnel measure had a bigger impact on final growth than on the more confounded dollar data. This study suggests that were all budget-based analyses of legislative-executive relations done on measures free of the mandated element that both the legislature and executive must bow to, legislatures would probably prove to be more independent of executives and more potent a force on agency requests.

In recent times additional evidence has emerged to show Congress breaking away from its traditional economizing role. Particularly in the social welfare area Congress has shifted from an economizing stance to an expansive posture. It has not been uncommon for Congress to add money to what the president has requested — so much so that the president has vetoed the Department of Labor and Department of Health, Education and Welfare Appropriations acts more than once in the 1970s.

The Congressional Budget Control and Impoundment Act of 1974 also heralds a change in feeling and perhaps in activity regarding budget matters on Capitol Hill. That act gives the Congress additional powers and expanded resources to pursue a more independent role. For fiscal year 1977, for example, Congress passed a budget spending ceiling of approximately $413 billion while the president's budget proposals did not at first exceed $400 billion. The coordinative powers that allowed Congress to set binding spending limits and that kept the membership to those limits came from the mechanisms set up in the 1974 legislation.

It must be reiterated that no comprehensive answer to the question of who is more powerful in the budget process will ever be possible. The roles assumed by people in the branches vary greatly, within the branches and over time. Even if there were uniformity in the roles, there still is a great degree of variety in how various agencies set requests, how committees treat them, and what is finally appropriated. Additional factors and influences over and above institutional roles and constraints must be considered.

PARTISAN EXPLANATIONS OF BUDGET POLITICS

Politics as the term has been used so far was spelled with a small "p." In this sense it referred to conflict that was not necessarily based on party. But the common interpretation of politics is colored by notions of formal political parties, the Republicans and the Democrats. Since much political activity is drawn along partisan lines, it is reasonable to inquire whether partisan politics intrudes into the budget process.

Unlike much governmental activity, party is not central to understanding budgeting. Appointment to executive policy positions is shot through with partisan considerations, and election to public office is usually achieved through the mediation of parties. Passage of the budget, however, is only moderately influenced by party considerations. At the federal level this is partly because of specialization and professionalization in Congress. Fenno has documented the position that the House Appropriations Committee is a workhorse committee that operates under largely nonpartisan norms.[4] The constant contact with the same kinds of problems and the same people demands that conflict be minimized in order to present a united committee face to the parent chamber. Little evidence therefore has been found of effective overt partisanship within Congress in approval of the budget requests. There is some evidence, however, that partisanship is coloring the behavior of some legislators in the budget resolutions required by the 1974 reform legislation.

On the other hand, in the relationship between Congress and the executive branch partisan factors have surfaced. One measure of the congeniality between the two branches is the percentage of the president's budget request that is approved by various congressional bodies. A high percentage indicates that there is an amicable budget relationship whereas a low percentage betokens conflict. If shifts of changes in this "success ratio" are associated with partisan differences or similarities in the Congress and the president, the impact of partisanship would be manifested.

Fenno's study of the budget experience of thirty-six domestic agencies indicates that partisan configuration influences budget congeniality between the branches. He computed the ratio of the House Appropriations Committee's budget recommendation to the president's requests over a number of years.[5] In 1947 the success rate was 76.1 percent; and in succeeding years it was 88.1 percent, 95.7 percent, 93.8 percent, 94.7 percent, 94.0 percent, and then dropped to 84.8 percent in 1953. The average range appears to be in the high eighties and low nineties. What happened in 1947 and 1953? In 1947 a Democratic president was presenting his budget to a newly elected Republican Congress and in 1953 a new Republican president was presenting a budget largely prepared by an outgoing Democrat to a newly elected Congress controlled by the Republicans. In the intervening years a Democratic Congress was acting on a budget from a Democratic president. The impact of partisanship here is obvious.

Difference in partisanship between the legislature and executive does not guarantee budgetary disagreement. In 1954 the success percentage was 95.1 percent, as one might expect when the same party controlled the White House and Capitol Hill. But in 1955, when the Democrats had control in Congress and Eisenhower was still president, the figure was still high at 97.3 percent; succeeding years recorded 96.3 percent, 92 percent, 99.5 percent, 99.6 percent, and 98.8 percent. It appears that Democratic Congresses are liberal with budgets proposed by Republicans but not vice versa. This anomaly is understandable if one realizes that Republicans typically try to keep government spending low and Democrats are more expansive. Republican-initiated budgets would therefore be viewed by Democrats as small to start out and little would be cut. But Democratic budgets would appear too large to Republican legislators who would, if their numbers allow, reduce the requests as much as possible.

It would be going beyond the data to argue that Democrats always try to spend and Republicans try to save. The ideological diversity found under the umbrella of either American party is too broad to warrant such a statement. The differences in orientation can merely be noted.

At the state level the partisan complexion of the legislature vis-à-vis the governor's mansion also seems to make a difference in budget relations. Building on the work of Sharkansky discussed earlier, Moncrief and Thompson asked whether the domination of the budget process by the governor was modified by party.[6] In the late 1960s and early 1970s they identified eight states where the governor's party enjoyed a legislative majority at one time but shifted to the situation where the governor's party was a minority. In the eight cases under study the gubernatorial dominance model described budget relations until the party change. In seven of the eight cases, when the governor's party no longer controlled the legislature, the model wherein both the governor and the agencies strongly influenced the legislature became dominant. Such a shift could have occurred by chance less than 5 percent of the time, which led Moncrief and Thompson to argue that the partisan complexion of the government has an important influence on budget outcomes.

Probably the most obvious area in which party politics influences budget outcomes lies in the formulation of the budget by the chief executive. Insofar as chief executives carry the party banner and embody the party's campaign platform, they will attempt to implement party preferences by means of budget proposals. A presidential candidate campaigning under party proposals for a stronger defense posture or cleaner air or lower crime rate will undoubtedly try to incorporate more money for the Pentagon, Environmental Protection Agency, or the FBI in the budget. Of course, the ability of a chief executive to propose a budget that implements party dogma is strongly constrained by revenue estimates and allowable deficits on the one side and uncontrollable commitments on the other. The latitude available for partisan-inspired budget proposals is always far less than desired.

CONTENT EXPLANATIONS OF BUDGET POLITICS

The explanations of budget outcomes so far have been content-free. Budget dollars have, in effect, been indistinguishable in that little attention has been paid to the purposes for which the money was intended. Certainly this is a bit simplistic. Since the budget process participants have differing goals and since money is often aimed at different clients or constituents, it is reasonable to expect that who gets what depends partly on "what" the money will buy.

It was just pointed out that money for mandated purposes — Medicare, veterans' benefits, Social Security, cost of living wage increases, or purchased items whose price has inflated — is generally proposed by the executive with little reticence and approved by the legislature with little hesitation. The nonmandatory or programmatic requests, however, will be treated differentially. Natchez and Bupp make this point quite clearly in the context of budget formulation in the Atomic Energy Commission.[7] They examined twenty-three programs carried on in the AEC from FY1958 through FY1972 and calculated a "prosperity score" that measures the relative success or failure of the programs competing for finances in the agency's budget request. Over that time period certain programs regularly were more prosperous than others. For example, programs on high-energy physics, nuclear safety, and general reactor technology were better off in money terms than programs on aircraft nuclear propulsion, army reactors, and training, education, and information. The nature of the programs was in some way responsible for the support that they garnered in budget formulation. High-level administrators preferred certain programs over others.

In the approval phase budget requests are also treated differentially depending on the programs included in the requests. Kanter's analysis of the Defense Department budgets from FY1960 through FY1970 demonstrated that Congress treated various titles of the defense appropriations bills with greater and lesser severity.[8] The four titles studied — personnel; operation and maintenance (O&M); procurement; and research, development, testing, and evaluation (RDT&E) — enjoyed different treatment. For one, Congress made fewer changes to the president's requests in personnel and O&M than it did in procurement and RDT&E. Second, the size of the changes in the budget requests were greater in procurement and RDT&E than in the other two titles. Because the procurement and RDT&E titles contain programs that set the direction of policies in the Defense Department, modification of those titles manifests an awareness of the programs involved and the differential impact of those programs on policy outputs.

On a much more specific level, it is well known that particular legislators often have pet projects or hobby horses they would like to see prosper. Congressman Fogarty, longtime chairman of the House Appropriations Subcommittee on the Departments of Labor and Health, Education and Welfare, was a strong advocate of medical research. He regularly added money to the budget requests made by medical research components of HEW because he felt those programs to be especially worthwhile. To other programs he supervised his actions were much more severe.

It is particularly difficult to specify what kinds of programs will be "hot items" in a budget and so get the full funding desired by the program managers. The successful Russian launching of Sputnik turned education programs into top-priority programs. In the mid-1970s education-related programs declined and energy-related programs enjoyed strong financial support. The important point to remember is that the substance of the budget request will be important in determining who supports the request and how strenuously they will stand behind it in budget formulation and approval.

STRATEGIC EXPLANATIONS OF BUDGET POLITICS

Much of budget politics is pictured as the conflict between the executive branch and the legislature. Bureaucratic expertise pitted against legislative representativeness might be the billing for politics in this arena. Since many of the participants are the same year after year, it is reasonable to expect that there will be attempts on the part of each actor to "psych out" the opposition. In short, strategies may be invoked to assist the agencies in maximizing their budgets and to aid the legislature in holding the line. This section presents some of the strategies and assesses the utility of a few of them.

Since the executive is trying to gain acquiescence from the legislature and has the first move, strategy will usually be examined from the point of view of the agencies. The most basic question that the agency asks is how much to request. The aggressiveness, acquisitiveness, or appetite of the request varies greatly from agency to agency. Does an aggressive demand or a modest request yield the most for the agency? No one answer can be given, although some patterns do appear.

In one sense a large appetite is a prerequisite for agency growth. Because legislatures rarely heap money on agencies over and above what they request, it is obvious that acquisitiveness is a necessary condition for budget growth. But is it sufficient? In most cases the answer is a qualified yes. Many studies have found a strong correlation between the increase requested and the increase appropriated. This high correlation occurs whether the analysis was done over time by specific agencies or across agencies. If you don't ask, you don't get.

The picture, however, is not simple. It also appears that agencies that request large increases over their previous base tend also to be cut the most. If the measure of the relationship between the branches is not the percentage increase in budget but the percentage of the request that was appropriated, there appears to be an inverse relationship. An agency that requests a small increase will probably receive a larger proportion of its request than an agency that asks for a large increase. In terms of the growth of the budget, however, there will be a larger increase experienced by the more aggressive agency than by the hesitant agency.

It would be prudent to remember that the choice of an expansive strategy may not be a wise or efficacious tactic. It would be laughable for an agency with a budget of $300,000 to ask for $5.2 million simply as a matter of strategy. An agency that asked for so much would lose any credibility it may have enjoyed with the legislature. It is also unlikely that an increase of that magnitude could be brought before a legislative body merely as a matter of tactics. Agency requests, it should be remembered, are reviewed by superordinate-level organizations like departments, central budget offices, and by the chief executive before they are presented to the legislature. If a very large request is made with the notion that large requests will guarantee a large appropriation, some or all of the reviewing stages in the budget formulation process will filter out much of the tactical padding, if only because such behavior reflects ill on the executive branch, which seeks to appear credible to the legislature.

Why then do some agencies get away with asking for larger increases than others? At least two factors come into play here: the merit of the requests and the nature of the agencies' constituencies. A frivolous request will probably be perceived as that, regardless of its size. If there is a genuine need for a program, an agency can plausibly seek larger amounts of money to implement the program. This, of course, does not guarantee that the request will be honored. In fact, it was noted that large requests tend to be cut heavily. But meritorious requests at least can be advanced.

The nature of the agencies' constituencies similarly allows agencies to be more aggressive in seeking large increases. If large numbers of people support an agency's programs, the pluralistic and group nature of our political system offers some assurance that such agencies can at least advance large requests because they know that their allies outside of the regular government budgeting participants will demand that their requests be taken seriously.

Research done by Ira Sharkansky nicely illustrates the relationship between acquisitive budget strategies on the part of the agencies and the nature of their constituents.[9] He examined the experiences from 1951 to 1963 of the Office of Education, the Children's Bureau, Howard University, and the Food and Drug Administration before the House Appropriations Subcommittee responsible for all of their requests. The Office of Education was by far the most aggressive in seeking funds while Howard University was downright timid. Because of Russia's launching of the first satellite, there was much concern about America's ability to do the same. Our educational system was thought to be partly at fault and educational institutions at all levels sought assistance to upgrade the quality of instruction. The Office of Education tried to act as the agency through which funds would be distributed to students, faculty, colleges, high schools, and other components of the educational establishment. It thereby represented and built up a very wide set of constituents. With such clout, the Office of Education could and did act quite aggressively in budgeting. Howard University, while an educational institution, had nowhere near that kind of outside support. Its clientele were blacks, and largely only blacks connected with that school. In numbers and in dispersion the constituents of Howard University were sparse. Without strong backing, budget presentations for that school were practically hat-in-hand and quite modest. Needless to say, even though the Office of Education's requests were cut more substantially than those of Howard University, because their requests were larger, they grew more.

DEMAND-BASED EXPLANATIONS OF BUDGET POLITICS

Earlier in the chapter budgeting was referred to as something of an insider's game. Most of the decision makers have been around for a long time, most know the other participants, few people are really involved, and there is a fair degree of regularity and predictability in budgetary interactions. This is what occurs in reality. In theory, however, the entire process is supposed to translate popular wishes into governmental action. Budget process participants, it must be admitted, do convey popular wishes into the forums of budgetary

decision making by a kind of institutional representation. Agriculture Department agencies press for what they perceive to be beneficial to farmers; Labor
Department agencies seek to advance the interests of the laborer; Commerce
Department agencies attempt to foster the well-being of the business commu-
nity. Similarly, the legislators on appropriations committees overseeing the
agencies represent the general popular interest in keeping spending down as
well as parochial desires for particular projects benefiting their districts. But
how do specific needs or demands explain particular budget decisions?

John E. Jackson's study of budgeting in Cleveland provides insight into the
impact of demand for services on budget decisions.[10] His research attempted,
among other things, to assess the applicability of both the bureaucratic model
and the economic or demand model of budgeting. The bureaucratic model
holds that it is the regularized and routinized interactions among the major
participants that generate discernible patterns in appropriations. The economic
or demand model predicts that external demands and needs for services determine how much will be allocated for various purposes. This latter model, for
example, would hold that the beginning of more new housing construction
would create a demand for greater appropriations for the city building inspection department. Likewise an increase in the crime rate would generate a demand for larger police budgets.

To summarize rather crudely Jackson's findings, elements of both models,
along with some political factors, were found to be important. In some spending
categories the demand or need for services was important in explaining how
much was appropriated. Sometimes demand was important under one mayor's
administration and not under other administrations. No univocal pattern of
spending emerged, but Jackson's study clearly showed that the need or demand
for specific spending is not a factor that can be ignored.

It should be obvious by now that the politics of passing the budget are
quite complex. In any one jurisdiction at any one time many of the forces
just sketched out would be operating. The complexity, however, does not reduce
the importance of the decision made in the budget process. The end result of
those decisions strongly influences what government does. To explore further
what government does in society today, the next chapter examines the outcomes of the budget process.

SUMMARY

Because budgeting allocates resources, budgeting is political. Basic explanations of budget politics are built on the notion of institutional role and constraint. Agencies are expected to be expansive, chief executives to be moderate, and legislatures to be economy oriented. Actions that would flow from those role expectations are, however, modified by various forces, such as uncontrollability outside the control of the actors. Understanding of these constraints modifies the common perception of the legislature as weaker than the executive branch.

Although partisanship does not seem to be important in explaining what goes on within each branch during the budget process, the partisan configuration of the executive and legislative branches does influence budgetary outcomes. Where the chief executive and the legislature bear the same party banner, much less conflict over the budget is likely to occur. Of course the partisan programs of chief executives are expressed in their budgets.

Similarly, the content of budgetary proposals has an effect on how much will be sought by the agencies as well as on how much the legislature will approve. Programmatic requests in the budget will be subjected to much more legislative scrutiny than mandated requests and, of course, the public visibility and topicality of programs will affect legislative treatment of requests for the funding.

Strategy appears to influence budget success insofar as an aggressive strategy employed by an agency generally means a large appropriation increase, but large requests are also likely to be cut a fair amount. Lastly, the impact of demand by outside clients seems to have an influence on budgetary outcomes under certain circumstances. These circumstances cannot easily be identified beforehand and their impact cannot be precisely predicted. Nonetheless they are important.

NOTES

1. Ira Sharkansky, "Agency Requests, Gubernatorial Support, and Budget Success in State Legislatures," *American Political Science Review* 62 (December 1968): 1220–1231.

2. John Wanat, "Bases of Budgetary Incrementalism," *American Political Science Review* 68 (September 1974): 1224–1228.

3. John Wanat, "Personnel Measures of Budgetary Interaction," *Western Political Quarterly* 29 (June 1976): 295–297.

4. Richard F. Fenno, Jr., "The House Appropriations Committee as a Political System: The Problem of Integration," *American Political Science Review* 56 (June 1962): 310–324.

5. Richard F. Fenno, Jr., *The Power of the Purse: Appropriations Politics in Congress* (Boston: Little, Brown, 1966), pp. 358–362.

6. Gary F. Moncrief and Joel A. Thompson, "Partisanship and Purse-Strings: A Research Note," mimeo, Department of Political Science, University of Kentucky, 1976.

7. Peter B. Natchez and Irvin C. Bupp, "Policy and Priority in the Budgetary Process," *American Political Science Review* 67 (September 1973): 951–963.

8. Arnold Kanter, "Congress and the Defense Budget, 1960–1970," *American Political Science Review* 66 (March 1972): 129–143.

9. Ira Sharkansky, "Four Agencies and an Appropriations Subcommittee: A Comparative Study of Budget Strategies," *Midwest Journal of Political Science* 9 (August 1965): 254–281.

10. John E. Jackson, "Politics and the Budgetary Process," *Social Science Research* 1 (1972): 35–60.

SELECTED BIBLIOGRAPHY

Cowart, Andrew R.; Hansen, Tore; and Brofoss, Karl-Erik. "Budgetary Strategies and Success at Multiple Decision Levels in the Norweigan Urban Setting." *American Political Science Review* 69 (June 1975): 543–558.

Cowart, Andrew T. "The Machiavellian Budgeter." *British Journal of Political Science* 6 (January 1976): 33–42.

_____. "Partisan Politics and the Budgetary Process in Oslo." *American Journal of Political Science* 19 (November 1975): 651–665.

Crecine, John P. *Governmental Problem Solving.* Chicago: Rand McNally, 1969.

Davis, David Howard. "The Price of Power: The Appropriations Process for Seventeen Foreign Affairs Agencies." *Public Policy* 18 (Spring 1970): 355–381.

Davis, Otto A.; Dempster, M. A. H.; and Wildavsky, Aaron. "A Theory of the Budgetary Process." *American Political Science Review* 60 (September 1966): 529–547.

_____. "On the Process of Budgeting: An Empirical Study of Congressional Appropriations." In *Papers on Non-Market Decision Making,* edited by Gordon Tullock. Charlottesville, Virginia: University of Virginia, 1966, pp. 63–132.

_____. "On the Process of Budgeting II: An Empirical Study of Congressional Appropriations." In *Studies in Budgeting,* edited by R. F. Byrne, A. Charnes, W. W. Cooper, O. A. Davis, and Dorothy Gilford. New York: North Holland Publishers, 1971.

_____. "Towards A Predictive Theory of Government Expenditures: U.S. Domestic Appropriations." *British Journal of Political Science* 4 (October 1974): 419–452.

Fenno, Richard F., Jr. "The House Appropriations Committee as a Political System: The Problem of Integration." *American Political Science Review* 56 (June 1962): 310–324.

_____. *The Power of the Purse: Appropriations Politics in Congress.* Boston: Little, Brown, 1966.

Ferejohn, John. *Pork Barrel Politics.* Berkeley: University of California Press, 1974.

Fisher, Lewis. *Presidential Spending Power.* Princeton, N.J.: Princeton University Press, 1975.

Hoole, Francis W. *Politics and Budgeting in the World Health Organization.* Bloomington: Indiana University Press, 1976.

Jackson, John E. "Politics and the Budgetary Process." *Social Science Research* 1 (1972): 35–60

Kanter, Arnold. "Congress and the Defense Budget, 1960–1970." *American Political Science Review* 66 (March 1972): 129–143.

Moncrief, Gary F., and Thompson, Joel A. "Partisanship and Purse-Strings: A Research Note." Mimeo, Department of Political Science, University of Kentucky, 1976.

Mosher, Frederick C., and Harr, John E. *Programming Systems and Foreign Affairs Leadership: An Attempted Innovation.* New York: Oxford University Press, 1970.

Natchez, Peter B., and Bupp, Irvin C. "Policy and Priority in the Budgetary Process." *American Political Science Review* 67 (September 1973): 951–963.

Nienaber, Jeanne, and Wildavsky, Aaron. *The Budgeting and Evaluation of Federal Recreation Programs, or Money Doesn't Grow on Trees.* New York: Basic Books, 1973.

Niskanen, William A. *Bureaucracy and Representative Government.* Chicago: Aldine-Atherton, 1971.

Schick, Allen. "The Battle of the Budget." In Harvey C. Mansfield, ed., *Congress Against the President, Proceedings of the Academy of Political Science* 32 (1975): 51–70.

Sharkansky, Ira. "Agency Requests, Gubernatorial Support, and Budget Success in State Legislatures." *American Political Science Review* 62 (December 1968): 1220–1231.

_____. "An Appropriations Subcommittee and Its Client Agencies." *American Political Science Review* 59 (September 1965): 622–628.

_____. "Four Agencies and an Appropriations Subcommittee: A Comparative Study of Budget Strategies." *Midwest Journal of Political Science* 9 (August 1965): 254–281.

Wanat, John. "Bases of Budgetary Incrementalism." *American Political Science Review* 68 (September 1974): 1221–1228.

_____. "Bureaucratic Politics in the Budget Formulation Process." *Administration and Politics* 7 (August 1975): 191–212.

_____. "Personnel Measures of Budgetary Interaction." *Western Political Quarterly* 29 (June 1976): 295–297.

Wildavsky, Aaron. "The Annual Expenditure Increment — or How Can Congress Regain Control of the Budget?" *The Public Interest* 33 (Fall 1973): 84–108.

_____. *Budgeting: A Comparative Theory of Budgetary Processes.* Boston: Little, Brown, 1975.

_____. *The Politics of the Budgetary Process,* 2nd ed. Boston: Little, Brown, 1974.

Chapter VIII

BUDGETS AS
EXPRESSIONS OF POLICY:

Where the

Money Goes

F eelings of bewilderment, powerlessness, and antagonism toward government are common. Some of these attitudes are traceable to the corruption and malfeasance of officeholders. But, while illegal and incompetent behavior does exist in government, most governmental action is both legal and competent. The generally negative feelings, it is suggested, are directly attributable to the remoteness and incomprehensibility of government activity.

The "anti-Washington" mood prevalent in the mid-1970s stands in curious contrast to the much more favorable attitudes toward state and local governments. In fact, some national-level politicians curry favor with their constituents by excoriating their colleagues who centralize and concentrate control in federal hands. They also engage in a rhetoric that promises decentralizing government by returning decision-making power to the cities, counties, and states. Relatively speaking, the citizenry accepts and welcomes local-level government as opposed to the national-level government because the more proximate government, among other things, appears to be understandable. The effects of one's tax payments can be seen in road repairs, new parks, improved schools, better social services, and similar tangible results. If governmental outputs are visible, they will be more comprehensible and therefore acceptable and, it is to be hoped, controllable to some extent. This is not to argue that on any absolute scale there will be rejoicing or even happy acceptance, merely that relative to the more distant and invisible governments, there will be less antagonism, bewilderment, and powerlessness. This comparison of levels of government illustrates the importance of understanding what government does for support of government.

Democratic theory requires that the citizenry understands what government does. One of the central tenets of democracy is accountability. If citizens are dissatisfied with the behavior of their government under the stewardship of elected officials, they vote to deny the incumbents their positions. However, this theory assumes that there is an enlightened electorate, that the populace knows what the government is and has been doing. In all too many cases the citizenry is ignorant of what government does. This means that elections become a farce insofar as voters cannot hold incumbents responsible for what they have done in proposing, supporting, and implementing government policies.

BUDGETS AS EXPRESSIONS OF PRIORITIES AND ACTIVITIES

How can a citizen grasp what a government is engaged in, given the large size of many units of government? As the introductory remarks have suggested, the answer to that question has important implications for popular attitudes toward and support for the political system as well as for the proper functioning of a democracy. This chapter argues that a government's budget is a useful and in some places the only means whereby a person can determine what is being done.

To put it rather baldly, budgets are a means by which a government puts its money where its mouth is. Since money is the lifeblood of agencies, tracing money allows assessing where the priorities are as well as merely seeing what the government is doing. The budget document presents in some detail money paid out in the past and requested for the future for every agency and, under some formats, for every activity and program. That document expresses the policies, in dollar terms, of the chief executive. The final appropriations bill (seen in next year's budget) expresses the legislature's judgment on what policies the government should engage in and the level of activity of each policy approved.

Many government jurisdictions recognize the utility of budgets for presenting what they do and the priorities to which they subscribe. Often the introductory sections of budget documents present summaries by activities, by functions, or by broad expenditure categories to give the reader a bird's-eye view of what the government is doing for them. The federal government publishes a pamphlet called *The Budget in Brief* to give an overview of the full budget and to explain simply to taxpayers where their money is going. Chief executives also take advantage of the budget submission to present their proposals for government activity for the upcoming budget year in the context of a public budget message. Of course, the full set of budget-related documents provides more than ample information on the specifics of governmental activities for most purposes.

It would be untenable to argue that budgets are a panacea for generating more favorable attitudes toward largely incomprehensible governments or for acting as a means to ensure accountability of elected officials. To be realistic, few people, even if they were aware of the utility of budgets for those purposes, would take advantage of them. But for the student of governmental phenomena, for the seriously civic-minded, and for the policy analyst the examination of budgets can generate important data on what government does and where tax monies are going. The remainder of this chapter is devoted to demonstrating how budgets can be used.

THE SCOPE OF GOVERNMENT: THE VIEW FROM THE BUDGET

One charge levied against government is its increasing size. Such a charge is understandable in a country that began in a struggle against governmental tyranny. The suspicion of rulers arising from the abuses of power that impelled the American colonists to break away from England found its way into the political culture of this nation. The self-sufficiency of the Jeffersonian yeoman has long been held out to the populace, first as the norm and lately as an ideal. The increasing size of government has been viewed as a threat to the independence of the individual idealized in the Jeffersonian yeoman.

To be sure, there must be some government. Chapter 2 clearly indicated that governmental activity is partly unavoidable because the market cannot provide all the services that society desires. However, much of what government provides is justified on the grounds that government should take over some of the functions from other societal actors. With the decline of the extended family system, for instance, there was the feeling that government should assume some of the responsibility for the elderly, the blind, the poor, and other less than self-sustaining segments of the population. Today there are people who feel that government has gone too far in intervening in the private sector. Others do not agree. Before any judgment can be made about either contention, data must be examined.

Because government activity is not free, examination of government spending will tell the analyst a great deal about government activity. And budgets will tell a great deal about government spending. Consider federal government spending. In fiscal year 1954 the government outlay was $70.9 billion; in fiscal year 1964 the outlay was $118.6 billion; by fiscal year 1974 spending was up to $268.4 billion.[1] Obviously governmental activity has increased substantially in that twenty-year period. Those who argue that government has expanded at an unreasonable rate would seem to have some substantiation for their claim.

Raw dollar figures must be considered carefully. For one, simply because there has been greater spending does not mean that the government has necessarily extended further into the private sector. The number of people taking advantage of government services may have increased at a rate proportional to the increase in government. In the case of the data just cited that probably is not the case. Certainly there has been nowhere near a threefold increase in the population and consequently it is unlikely that a threefold increase was necessary to meet the demand created by changes in the demography of society. Yet demographic changes must be considered and some of the increased spending is justifiable because of changes in, for example, the number of people claiming a service.

To control for changes in the size of the relevant populations, the notion of the gross national product is useful. By investigating the proportion of the GNP represented by the national budget it is possible to assess the involvement in or the penetration of government into the whole of society. In the period from FY1954 through FY1974 the ratio of federal budget outlays has averaged 19.5 percent, never going below 17.2 percent or rising above 21.6 percent.[2] This contrasts strongly with popular notions that the federal government has on the fiscal front increasingly expanded into the private realm in the recent past.

Another finding from the analysis of federal budgets also contrasts with folklore. Concern with deficit spending and the increasing yearly deficits engenders the notion that federal spending is disproportionately large. As a matter of fact, although the raw size of the federal debt generally increases from year to year, total federal debt as a percentage of the GNP has dropped in the recent past. From FY1954, when the debt was equivalent to 74.8 percent of the GNP, that index has dropped in a fairly regular manner to the point where in FY1974 the figure was only about 36 percent.[3]

To be fair, it must be noted that over a longer period of time federal government spending as a percentage of GNP has increased. In FY1902 the figure was only 3.2 percent, by FY1922 it had risen to 5.9 percent, in FY1942 it reached 11.6 percent and then has stayed fairly stable since the 1950s.[4]

At the state and local levels, however, folkloric notions of expanding government are borne out using spending data. Not only have raw expenditures and raw growth been occurring, but as a percentage of the GNP an increase has been apparent. State and local spending as a percentage of GNP was 5 percent in FY1902; it was 6.9 percent in FY1922, 8.8 percent in FY1942, 11.4 percent in FY1962, and 14.4 percent in FY1972.[5]

While some light has been shed in this section on popular ideas about the scope of governmental activity, the major point is that budgets form the tool by which governmental activity can be assessed, not the only tool to be sure, but still a very valuable and comprehensive one.

BUDGETS AND GOVERNMENTAL PRIORITIES

Compared to twenty years ago the study of governmental activity has shifted its focus rather dramatically. Perhaps because of a dominating concern for responsiveness and for democratic participation in governing, analysts of government focused heavily on the input side of government. That is to say, great attention was paid to voting behavior, to interest group behavior, to legislative behavior, to recruitment patterns to political life, and to other concerns centering on how policies were established for the first time. It was as if the only thing that counted was the passage of the law or the handing down of the Supreme Court decisions. Once that was done, implementation was taken for granted.

Unfortunately, the input-oriented focus gives a misleading picture of governmental activity for two reasons. First, concentration on the new law, the new decision, the new ruling through case studies, roll call analysis, or any other technique frequently ignores the vast bulk of old law, old decisions, and old rulings that still apply and that still influence and bind the governmental apparatus and so the citizenry. Concerted study of novel phenomena is bound to distort the perspective that is essential to full understanding of government.

Second, focusing on the input side of government tells practically nothing about what really counts, the delivery of the goods. Just because Congress passes a law does not mean that its intent will be carried out. Just because the Supreme Court issues a precedent-breaking opinion does not guarantee that it will be observed by lower courts and law enforcement agencies. To use the old cliché, there is many a slip twixt the cup and the lip. Analysts of government should be interested in what is imbibed and not solely in the contents of the cup.

More recently some social scientists studying government have shifted their orientation to what has broadly been called policy studies. They are interested in what government actually does for or to the citizenry. Their emphasis is on the outputs of the governmental apparatus, mostly the executive branch mechanisms that attempt to implement the decisions made. They attempt to measure the impact of the decision made in, say, the legislatures on the ultimate recipients or the targets of the policy.

One tool or source of data frequently utilized by policy analysts is government expenditure data taken from budgets. For one who wishes to get a perspective on what a governmental apparatus is doing examination of the expenditures as spelled out in a budget document is sure to provide a great deal of raw material for study inasmuch as every penny must be spelled out. The relative commitment of an administration to various programs and policies is, after a little comparison, visible to all. Not only are the programs that make news in the budget, but the programs that go on and on in relative obscurity are there, too.

It is a bit hard to argue that the impact of a program can be measured solely by the amount of money spent in the program. But it certainly is true that there is some connection between spending for programs and the provision of some level of service. More on this will be said later. This section now turns to a simple illustration or two of how budgets can be used to identify priorities in government programs and to trace changes in governmental priorities and programs.

Table 8.1 displays the percentage breakdown of spending according to functional areas over a period of some thirty-five years for the federal government. The figures for 1976 clearly demonstrate that as a nation our greatest concern appears to be for income security inasmuch as most of the budget will be expended to that end. Indeed, analysis of federal budgets over time indicates that there has been an increasingly strong commitment to social policies. Income security accounted for only 13.7 percent of the budget in 1941, a figure that almost tripled by 1976. Another important trend that emerges is the decreasing priority given to defense spending. While it has been greater than social welfare spending for the longest time, it is now eclipsed by social welfare programs. This is not to say that the defense establishment is on very hard times. In absolute dollars it has grown year after year. Table 8.1 only portrays the percentage distribution of the total budget.

Budgets can also be useful to illustrate differences in priorities across national boundaries. Table 8.2 presents money expended by a select group of nations for three purposes as a percentage of those nations' gross national product. The data in the table indicate the emphasis those countries put on public education, public health, and military affairs in 1970. The very range of the data is illuminating. There is much greater variation in the military

*TABLE 8.1. PERCENTAGE DISTRIBUTION OF FEDERAL BUDGET OUT-
LAYS BY FUNCTION.*

FUNCTION	1941	1946	1951	1956	1961	1966	1971	1976 EST
National defense	44.3	75.3	47.8	56.4	47.6	41.5	36.3	26.9
International affairs	1.1	3.5	8.2	3.4	3.3	3.4	1.5	1.8
General science, space, and technology	.1	.1	.2	.2	1.1	5.0	2.0	1.3
Natural resources, environment, and energy	6.4	.9	3.1	1.5	2.2	2.3	2.1	2.9
Agriculture	2.5	1.1	—.7	4.9	2.7	1.8	2.0	.5
Commerce and transportation	4.7	.1	4.8	2.8	5.3	6.7	4.9	3.9
Community and regional development	1.1	.4	.6	.3	.5	1.1	1.9	1.7
Education, manpower, and social services	12.5	.2	.5	.8	1.1	3.0	4.3	4.2
Health	.4	.4	.7	.5	.9	2.0	7.0	8.0
Income security	13.7	4.7	10.2	14.0	21.9	21.5	26.2	34.0
Veterans benefits and services	4.1	4.5	12.1	7.1	5.8	4.4	4.6	4.5
Law enforcement and justice	.7	.3	.5	.4	.4	.4	.6	.9
General government	2.2	1.6	2.3	.7	1.1	1.1	1.0	.9
Revenue sharing and general purpose fiscal assistance	.1	a	.1	.1	.2	.2	.2	2.1
Interest	8.1	8.5	12.2	8.9	8.3	8.4	9.3	9.9
Allowances	——	——.	——	——	——	——	——	2.3
Undistributed offsetting receipts	—1.9	—1.5	—2.6	—2.1	—2.5	—2.7	—4.0	—5.8
Total outlays	100.0	100.0	100.0	100.0	100.0	100.0	100.0	100.0

SOURCE: U.S., Executive Office of the President, Office of Management and Budget,
  The Budget In Brief, Fiscal Year 1976, Washington, D.C.: Government
  Printing Office, 1975, p. 66.
a. Less than 0.05%

TABLE 8.2. EXPENDITURES FOR MILITARY, PUBLIC EDUCATION, AND PUBLIC HEALTH IN SELECTED COUNTRIES AS A PERCENTAGE OF GNP, 1970.

COUNTRY	MILITARY	PUBLIC EDUCATION	PUBLIC HEALTH
Burma	5.8	3.12	1.06
Cambodia	16.6	4.74	1.05
Canada	2.2	8.22	3.36
China (Mainland)	8.3	5.00	0.22
Colombia	1.4	3.18	1.70
Cuba	5.6	8.13	1.19
Denmark	2.4	5.71	5.45
Egypt	1.5	2.96	1.11
Finland	1.4	6.75	4.28
France	4.0	4.13	0.23
India	3.4	2.50	0.67
Jordan	20.5	4.00	1.04
North Korea	15.6	3.00	0.33
Mexico	0.7	2.46	1.21
Netherlands	3.5	6.59	3.87
Pakistan	3.7	1.20	0.59
Portugal	7.0	1.44	1.61
Syria	13.8	3.27	0.50
Turkey	4.6	4.44	1.16
United Kingdom	4.8	4.65	4.47
United States	8.0	5.57	2.75
North Vietnam	20.0	7.67	1.33
South Vietnam	34.0	2.00	0.81

SOURCE: U.S. Arms Control and Disarmament Agency, *World Military Expenditures, 1970* (Washington, D.C., GPO, 1972), pp. 10–13. Some inaccuracies may be expected in the table because basic data in some cases are estimates.

expenditures than in either public education or public health, largely because of the war or near-war situations in some countries. Even in health and education, however, some countries (Denmark, Canada, and Finland, for example) are ahead of most of the rest.

What explains the changing priority given to social welfare policies in this country or the relative importance of education and health programs in other countries will not be found in budget documents. But the raw data describing the variation will.

The point of this chapter has been to emphasize that budgets can serve to present what a government is engaged in as well as to indicate the priorities of a regime. Budgets, however, cannot be assumed to give absolute and unequivocal data at all times. A few qualifications are in order.

As conservatives have argued for quite a while, just because money is spent does not mean that results will be forthcoming in direct proportion to the spending. It is not justifiable to equate budget expenditures with substantial results. Spending money for schools does not guarantee that students will be functionally literate. Spending money for public health programs does not inevitably lead to better health. Higher police salaries do not ensure lower crime rates. Ira Sharkansky has shown that at the state level there is not often a strong connection between spending for a given purpose and more "substantial" measures of progress toward that purpose.[6] This is to be expected since causality is a complex phenomenon. Merely paying teachers more money will not necessarily imbue them with fervor, guarantee that they will be well trained, or enhance students' instruction. In short, inputs do not guarantee outcomes, and money is a kind of input. However, there will probably be a closer connection between money inputs to a program and the outcomes of the program than there will be between the bare enabling statute and the outcomes of the programs. Some money, after all, is a necessary if not a sufficient condition for programmatic success.

Even if money cannot be viewed as measuring the effective impact of programs, it should be considered an excellent measure of intentions and symbolic action. Money budgeted for education may not create literate seventh graders, but it serves to show that the government is attempting to stamp out illiteracy and is symbolic of executive branch attempts. The older studies of government looked at symbolic action in the passage of laws that instituted programs; budgets get at the symbolic actions of the executive branch.

A second fact that must temper enthusiasm about using budgets to measure the priorities of, say, various administrations is the uncontrollability of much of the budget. The budget presented by a given administration to the legislature is probably set to a large degree by previous legislation and expectations regarding ongoing programs. Prior commitments constitute much of any budget. It must be remembered, however, that budgets change in both size and composition. Policy priorities of particular regimes will be visible at the margins, that is, in the changes from the previous budget. Changes in the margins turn out, as time passes, to have an impact on the composition of the base budget. The rise in social welfare spending in the federal budget did not necessarily occur at the expense of other spending programs; social welfare spending simply got a larger piece of the increase year after year and so became the largest spending category in the budget. Likewise, the drop in the proportion of spending for national defense was not a reduction in absolute spending. Thus, while budgets give an accurate picture of spending priorities, those priorities cannot necessarily be attributed to the administration that proposes the budget, although changes from the previous budget can be indicative of short-term priorities.

SUMMARY

Budgets are useful in assessing the scope of government, the nature of its activities, and the priorities of any administration. Consequently, budgets are a means by which the citizenry can hold its government accountable. For example, analysis of budget size over time by itself and in relation to total economic activity indicates that the government has indeed grown substantially, although not always in the way popular opinion holds. Analysis of budget size relative to economic activity indicates that even though the federal government has grown substantially in the last twenty years, it has remained a relatively constant proportion of total economic activity, even though popular opinion says that the federal government has grown disproportionately. In actuality over the last twenty years the greatest growth in government spending has occurred at the state and local levels.

The composition of budgets also indicates which programs are favored by various administrations and when studied over time show trends in government priorities. At the federal level, for example, the greater attention given to social welfare programs is clearly manifest in the larger proportion of the budget going into that area.

Even though expenditures may not be ideal measures of government activity and are certainly not very good measures of actual government output, they still retain their power as indicators of executive desires. Budgets, consequently, also measure symbolic outputs of government.

NOTES

1. Office of Management and Budget, Executive Office of the President, *The United States Budget in Brief, Fiscal Year 1976* (Washington, D.C.: Government Printing Office, 1975), table 8.

2. Ibid.

3. Ibid.

4. Roger A. Freeman, *The Growth of American Government,* (Stanford, California: Hoover Institution Press, Stanford University, 1975), p. 203.

5. Ibid.

6. Ira Sharkansky, "Government Expenditures and Public Services in the American States," *American Political Science Review* 61 (December 1967): 1066–1077.

SELECTED BIBLIOGRAPHY

Coleman, Kenneth M., and Wanat, John. "On Measuring Mexican Presidential Ideology Through Budgets." *Latin American Research Review* 10 (Spring 1975): 77–88.

Derthick, Martha. *Uncontrollable Spending for Social Services.* Washington, D.C.: The Brookings Institution, 1975.

Freeman, Roger A. *The Growth of American Government: A Morphology of the Welfare State.* Stanford, California: Hoover Institution Press, Stanford University, 1975.

Kanter, Arnold. "Congress and the Defense Budget, 1960–1970." *American Political Science Review* 66 (March 1972): 129–143.

Natchez, Peter B., and Bupp, Irvin C. "Policy and Priority in the Budgetary Process." *American Political Science Review* 67 (September 1973): 931–963.

Ripley, Randall B., and Franklin, Grace A., eds. *Policy-Making in the Federal Executive Branch.* New York: Free Press, 1975.

Sharkansky, Ira. "Government Expenditures and Public Services in the American States." *American Political Science Review* 61 (December 1967): 1066–1077.

——. *The Politics of Taxing and Spending.* Indianapolis: Bobbs-Merrill, 1969.

U.S. Arms Control and Disarmament Agency. *World Military Expenditures, 1970.* Washington, D.C.: Government Printing Office, 1972.

U.S., Executive Office of the President, Office of Management and Budget. *The United States Budget in Brief, Fiscal Year 1976.* Washington, D.C.: Government Printing Office, 1975.

U.S., Executive Office of the President, Office of Management and Budget. *Special Analyses, Budget of the United States Government, Fiscal Year 1976.* Washington, D.C.: Government Printing Office, 1975.

Appendix

Document 1: Budget Preparation Instructions*

INSTRUCTIONS: CURRENT OPERATING EXPENDITURES

Agency requests for operating expenses must consolidate current program obligations and planned program requirements. Biennial cost estimates for commodities, supplies, grant and benefit payments should be based on present unit prices unless specifically noted otherwise. Cost estimates for each minor code must be recorded by budget unit in the appropriate spaces on ATTACHMENT 3 and certain expenditures itemized on the SCHEDULES as indicated in the Appendix (blue pages).

Code 301 -

Postage, Freight, and Express. Enter budget estimates for postal cards, stamps, stamped envelopes, postage meters, and parcel post, freight, railway express, and local truck hauling service when such items cannot be directly charged to the appropriate commodity or service. All mail and freight rates must be calculated as follows:

a. First class mail. Agencies may assume a maximum of 33 percent increase each year of the biennium using an estimated proportion of their total budgeted 301 figure for the base year 1971–72.

b. Second class mail. Agencies may assume a maximum of 28.4 percent increase each year of the biennium using an estimated proportion of their total budgeted 301 figure for the base year 1971–72.

c. Third class mail. Agencies may assume a maximum of 6.6 percent increase each year of the biennium using an estimated proportion of their total budgeted 301 figure for the base year 1971–72.

d. Freight, local truck, or hauling service rates. Agencies may assume a maximum increase of 4 percent the first year and 5 percent the second year over the base year 1971–72.

Code 302 -

Telephone and Telegraph. Record budget estimates for regular monthly bills for local telephone service including charges for centrex; regular monthly bills for long distance service; payments for telegraph, teletype, cable or related messenger service; and other tele-communication services. Agency requests will assume existing rates.

*Source: Commonwealth of Kentucky, Department of Finance, Division of the Budget, *Budget Request Manual,* 1971, pp. 5–6.

Code 303 -

Care and Support. Record budget estimates for room, laboratory, operating room, food and related charges made by a hospital for the care of patients; attending physicians' charges for inpatient and outpatient services; charges incurred by educational institutions for injured athletes; room, food, and other charges for maintenance and care in private homes whether the charges are on a contractual basis or a rate computed on a daily, weekly, or monthly basis; charges for maintenance and care of children in a day nursery whether the charges are on a contractual basis or on a rate computed daily, weekly, or monthly; and payments for the care, feeding, and maintenance of wards of the state not otherwise classified above. Agency requests must include existing rate schedules and identify and justify all proposed revisions in rate computations. Existing and proposed service levels (case load statistics) must also be enumerated in the narrative for each fiscal year in the new biennium.

Code 304 -

Intrastate Travel and Subsistence. Record Budget estimates for all transportation, mileage, hotel or motel, meals, registration and other necessary expenses incurred by officials or authorized employees in attending official meetings, conferences, or in otherwise performing their official duties within the confines of the state. Agency requests must assume existing eight cents per mile reimbursement rate for use of private vehicles. Agency mileage cost projections should be weighed and balanced against requests for new and replacement vehicles (Code 605) in the new biennium and the utilization of central and agency motor pools. Travel requests must further be tempered by prudent administration of travel regulations.

Code 305 -

Printing and Advertising. Record budget estimates for newspaper, magazine, and other advertisements in connection with bids and sales; pamphlets, cuts, printing of special reports and binding, and other promotional advertising, total charges made for printing and paper and other costs involved where one state agency provides this service for another agency. Agency requests may assume 8 percent increase each year of the biennium over the current level.

Code 306 -

Utilities. Record budget estimates for electricity, natural gas, water, sewage, and other utilities provided by commercial services. Agency requests may assume a 12 percent increase in existing rates in each year of the new biennium.

Document 2: Budget Preparation Instructions*

OBJECT CLASSIFICATION—WITH ALLOCATION ACCOUNTS

PY - past year
CY - current year
BY - budget year

STANDARD FORM **304**
May 1960. Bureau of the Budget
Circular No. A-11, Revised
304-105

DEPARTMENT OF GOVERNMENT
BUREAU OF PUBLIC WORKS
CONSTRUCTION
OBJECT CLASSIFICATION (in thousands of dollars)

Type size:
8 point 22 picas
Case 180;
Re-1 underscore
Case 210

Standard Form 300 may be used at the option of the agency in lieu of Standard Form 304 when it is more convenient. When Standard Form 300 is used, the applicable entries will follow the format of the preprinted form to the fullest extent possible and be coded the same as on Standard Form 304.

Identification code 16-50-3044-0-1-452		19 PY actual	19 CY estimate	19 BY estimate
BUREAU OF PUBLIC WORKS				
Personnel compensation:				
11.1	Permanent positions	20,965	34,056	35,979
11.3	Positions other than permanent	156	207	220
11.5	Other personnel compensation	1,079	1,817	1,910
11.8	Special personal services payments			
	Total personnel compensation	22,200	36,080	38,099
	Personnel benefits:			
12.1	Civilian	979	1,505	1,612
13.0	Benefits for former personnel			
21.0	Travel and transportation of persons	307	395	409
	Total costs, funded	40,001	46,000	47,191
94.0	Change in selected resources	-6,827	4,899	6,871
XXX	Total obligations, Bureau of Public Works	33,174	50,899	54,062

OBJECT CLASSIFICATION (in thousands of dollars)   p. 2

Where there is only one allocation or allotment, the center heading and the total line will contain the name of the organizational unit involved and the distribution below will be omitted.

Identification code 16-50-3044-0-1-452		19 PY actual	19 CY estimate	19 BY estimate
ALLOCATION ACCOUNTS				
Personnel compensation:				
11.1	Permanent positions	450	705	690
11.3	Positions other than permanent	6	12	9
11.5	Other personnel compensation	1	5	2
11.8	Special personal services payments			
	Total personnel compensation	456	722	701
	Personnel benefits:			
12.1	Civilian	20	29	27

This entry will agree with the total obligations on the program and financing schedule.

	Total obligations, allocation accounts	691	994	924
99.0	Total obligations	33,865	51,893	54,986

Obligations are distributed as follows:

The parent organizational unit will be listed first, followed, as applicable, by (a) other bureaus within the same agency, and (b) other agencies in budget order.

Bureau of Public Works	33,174	50,899	54,062
Bureau of Inspection	450	610	515
Department of the Interior	40	47	47
General Services Administration	201	337	362

PERSONNEL SUMMARY

Identification code 16-50-3044-0-1-452	19 PY actual	19 CY estimate	19 BY estimate
BUREAU OF PUBLIC WORKS			
Total number of permanent positions	3,450	4,800	4,950
Full-time equivalent of other positions	7	6	6
ALLOCATION ACCOUNTS			
Total number of permanent positions	69	100	95
Full-time equivalent of other positions	1	1	0

The average grade and salary will be the weighted average of the grades and salaries reported by the receiving agencies.

Average GS grade	7.6	7.9	7.8
Average GS salary	$6,769	$7,388	$7,105

*Source: U.S., Executive Office of the President, Bureau of the Budget, "Preparation and Submission of Annual Budget Estimates (June, 1970)," Circular No. A-11, Revised, p. 178.

Document 3: Portion of Federal Budget*

Program and Financing (in thousands of dollars)

	1961 actual	1962 estimate	1963 estimate
Program by activities:			
1. Assessment and collection of duties, taxes, and fees	39,086	41,277	42,019
2. Appraisal of imported merchandise	9,557	10,109	10,500
3. Investigations of violations of customs and related laws and regulations	6,719	7,084	8,648
4. Audit of collection and merchandise accounts	873	1,001	1,027
5. Analysis and identification of merchandise for tariff purposes	1,242	1,330	1,340
6. Executive direction	2,317	2,429	2,466
Total program costs[1]	59,793	63,231	66,000
Change in selected resources[2]	−14		
Total obligations	59,779	63,231	66,000
Financing:			
Unobligated balance brought forward	300	300	300
Unobligated balance carried forward	−300	−300	−300
Unobligated balance lapsing	36		
New obligational authority	**59,815**	**63,231**	**66,000**
New obligational authority:			
Appropriation	59,815	63,325	66,000
Transferred to "Operating expenses, Public Buildings Service," General Services Administration (75 Stat. 353)		−94	
Appropriation (adjusted)	**59,815**	**63,231**	**66,000**

[1] Includes capital outlay as follows: 1961, $216 thousand; 1962, $225 thousand; 1963, $225 thousand.

[2] Selected resources as of June 30 are as follows:

	1960	1961 adjustments	1961	1962	1963
Stores	28	-----	21	21	21
Unpaid undelivered orders	298	−2	291	288	291
Advances	4	-----	1	4	1
Total selected resources	330	−2	313	313	313

*Source: U.S., *The Budget of the United States Government, Fiscal Year Ending June 30, 1963 - Appendix*, Washington, D.C.: Government Printing Office, 1962, pp. 633-634.

BUREAU OF CUSTOMS

Current authorizations:

SALARIES AND EXPENSES

For necessary expenses of the Bureau of Customs, including purchase of [sixty] *one hundred* passenger motor vehicles (*of which seventy-five shall be* for replacement only [, of which forty]) *including eighty* for police-type use *which* may exceed by $300 each the general purchase price limitation for the current fiscal year; uniforms or allowances therefor, as authorized by the Act of September 1, 1954, as amended (5 U.S.C. 2131); services as authorized by section 15 of the Act of August 2, 1946 (5 U.S.C. 55a); and awards of compensation to informers as authorized by the Act of August 13, 1953 (22 U.S.C. 401); [$62,650,000] *$66,000,000.*

[For an additional amount for "Salaries and expenses", $675,000.] *(5 U.S.C. 118, 118a, 281a; 19 U.S.C. 68, 1524, 1619, 1701; 31 U.S.C. 529b, 530; 46 U.S.C. 1–1334; Treasury-Post Office Appropriation Act, 1962; Supplemental Appropriation Act, 1962.)*

The Bureau of Customs collects the duties and taxes on imported merchandise, inspects all international traffic, regulates certain marine and aircraft activities, combats smuggling, undervaluation, and frauds on the customs revenue, and performs related functions in connection with the importation and exportation of merchandise.

Direct obligations are estimated to be $66,000 thousand for 1963, an increase of $2,675 thousand over the amount now appropriated for 1962.

The unobligated balance of $300 thousand is a special fund available to this account when necessary to help pay the expenses of reimbursable customs work pending the collection of receivables from private interests.

1. *Assessment and collection of duties, taxes, and fees.* —The collectors of customs assess and collect the duties and taxes on imported merchandise, inspect international traffic, combat smuggling, perform certain marine activities relating to ownership and documentation of vessels of the United States and the movement of vessels in the foreign trade, and enforce the laws of other Government agencies affecting imports and exports.

SELECTED WORKLOAD DATA

[In thousands]

	1960 actual	*1961 actual*	*1962 estimate*	*1963 estimate*
Formal entries accepted _ _ _ _ _ _ _ _ _	1,476	1,398	1,400	1,400
Carriers of persons and merchandise arriving from foreign countries _ _ _	43,621	45,176	46,983	48,862
Persons arriving from foreign countries	149,643	158,386	164,700	171,300

2. *Appraisal of imported merchandise.* —The customs appraisers examine and ascertain the value of imported merchandise, and perform other functions in support of the collectors' determinations of rates of duty to be assessed and the admissibility of merchandise into the United States.

SELECTED WORKLOAD DATA

[In thousands]

	1960 actual	1961 actual	1962 estimate	1963 estimate
Packages examined _ _ _ _ _ _ _ _ _ _ _ _	1,386	1,377	1,380	1,380
Packages sampled _ _ _ _ _ _ _ _ _ _ _ _ _	(¹)	303	305	305
Invoices received _ _ _ _ _ _ _ _ _ _ _ _ _	2,322	2,181	2,180	2,180

[1] Not available.

3. *Investigations of violations of customs and related laws and regulations.*—The customs agents in the United States and abroad make investigations in the enforcement of the Tariff Act of 1930, the Narcotics Drug Act of 1934, the Gold Reserve Act of 1934, the Export Control Act, and other laws affecting the movement of merchandise into and out of the United States. They also secure market value information for customs appraisers. In 1961, 18,828 investigations were made. The estimates for 1962 and 1963 are 19,915 and 20,365, respectively.

4. *Audit of collection and merchandise accounts.*—The comptrollers of customs examine and certify collectors' accounts of receipts and disbursements of money and receipts and disposition of merchandise, and verify collectors' final assessments of duties and taxes, as well as allowances of drawback.

SELECTED WORKLOAD DATA

	1960 actual	1961 actual	1962 estimate	1963 estimate
Liquidations verified _ _ _ _ _ _ _ _ _ _ _	80,503	80,035	95,000	95,000
Comptrollers verifications pending at close of year _ _ _ _ _ _ _ _ _ _ _ _ _ _ _	2,153	6,790	3,500	3,500
Audit reports made _ _ _ _ _ _ _ _ _ _ _ _	142	119	125	125

5. *Analysis and identification of merchandise for tariff purposes.*—The customs laboratories perform scientific analysis and identification of merchandise for tariff and enforcement purposes. In 1961, 122,543 samples were tested, and it is estimated that 130,000 and 131,650 will be tested in 1962 and 1963, respectively.

APPENDIX TO THE BUDGET FOR FISCAL YEAR 1963

BUREAU OF CUSTOMS—Continued

Current authorizations—Continued

SALARIES AND EXPENSES—Continued

6. *Executive direction.*—The Washington office of the Bureau of Customs directs, unifies, and controls the functioning of the customs service.

Object Classification (in thousands of dollars)

	1961 actual	1962 estimate	1963 estimate
11 Personnel compensation:			
Permanent positions	49,166	51,882	54,100
Positions other than permanent	459	475	509
Other personnel compensation	2,229	2,226	2,400
Total personnel compensation	51,853	54,583	57,009
12 Personnel benefits	4,431	4,667	4,886
21 Travel and transportation of persons	616	747	902
22 Transportation of things	487	519	520
23 Rent, communications, and utilities	753	833	826
24 Printing and reproduction	165	201	171
25 Other services	350	360	324
26 Supplies and materials	465	473	488
31 Equipment	460	642	667
32 Lands and structures	216	225	225
42 Insurance claims and indemnities	8	8	8
Subtotal	59,804	63,257	66,026
Deduct quarters and subsistence charges	25	26	26
Total obligations	59,779	63,231	66,000

Personnel Summary

Total number of permanent positions	7,498	7,730	8,070
Full-time equivalent of other positions	93	96	102
Average number of all employees	7,328	7,637	7,968
Number of employees at end of year	7,604	8,000	8,286
Average GS grade	8.2	8.4	8.3
Average GS salary	$6,887	$7,030	$7,081
Average salary of ungraded positions	$5,202	$5,231	$5,253

Permanent authorizations:

REFUNDS AND DRAWBACKS, CUSTOMS

(Indefinite)

Program and Financing (in thousands of dollars)

	1961 actual	1962 estimate	1963 estimate
Program by activities:			
Assessment and collection of duties, taxes, and fees (total program costs—obligations) (object class 44)	25,439	25,500	25,500
Financing:			
New obligational authority (appropriation)	**25,439**	**25,500**	**25,500**

Overpayments are refunded, and drawback of duties upon exportation of previously imported merchandise are paid as required.

Intragovernmental funds:

ADVANCES AND REIMBURSEMENTS

Program and Financing (in thousands of dollars)

	1961 actual	1962 estimate	1963 estimate
Program by activities:			
1. Assessment and collection of duties, taxes, and fees	10,058	11,408	11,893
2. Appraisal of imported merchandise	223	249	249
3. Investigations of violations of customs and related laws and regulations	212	249	249
5. Analysis and identification of merchandise for tariff purposes		1	1
6. Executive direction	44	45	45
Total obligations	10,537	11,950	12,435

	1961 actual	1962 estimate	1963 estimate
Financing:			
Advances and reimbursements from—			
Other accounts	2,641	2,974	3,109
Non-Federal sources	7,896	8,976	9,326
Total financing	10,537	11,950	12,435

Note.—Reimbursements from non-Federal sources above are funds received for overtime pay and miscellaneous expenses for customs services (19 U.S.C. 1524).

Object Classification (in thousands of dollars)

		1961 actual	1962 estimate	1963 estimate
11	Personnel compensation:			
	Permanent positions	3,830	4,139	4,262
	Positions other than permanent	50	50	50
	Other personnel compensation	6,096	7,095	7,445
	Total personnel compensation	9,976	11,284	11,757
12	Personnel benefits	190	216	228
21	Travel and transportation of persons	110	138	138
22	Transportation of things	6	6	6
23	Rent, communications, and utilities	19	19	19
24	Printing and reproduction	104	105	105
25	Other services	25	26	26
26	Supplies and materials	11	12	12
31	Equipment	23	24	24
32	Lands and structures	73	120	120
	Total obligations	10,537	11,950	12,435

Personnel Summary

	1961 actual	1962 estimate	1963 estimate
Total number of permanent positions	719	750	780
Full-time equivalent of other positions	10	10	10
Average number of all employees	663	720	745
Number of employees at end of year	682	707	732
Average GS grade	7.3	7.3	7.4
Average GS salary	$6,064	$6,219	$6,326
Average salary of ungraded positions	$5,049	$5,214	$5,257

Document 4: Portion of U.S. Senate Appropriations Committee Report*

OCCUPATIONAL SAFETY AND HEALTH ADMINISTRATION

SALARIES AND EXPENSES

1972 funds available	$35,884,000
1973 budget estimate.	69,207,000
House allowance	69,207,000
Committee recommendation	80,000,000

The Committee recommends $80,000,000, an increase of $10,793,000 over the House allowance and the budget estimate. The additional funds are to be used to employ approximately 400 additional compliance officers to develop health and safety standards, and to help small business and unorganized employees cope with new developments and standards in the occupational safety and health field.

This is a new appropriation to finance a full year's operation of the Occupational Safety and Health Administration established to carry out the provisions of the Occupational Safety and Health Act of 1970. Costs in the amount of $35,884,000 were financed in 1972 in the appropriation for the Workplace Standards Administration (which was redesignated as the Employment Standards Administration). The 1973 budget estimate provides for full-year costs of new positions authorized in 1972, the establishment of advisory committees to develop safety and health standards, increases in compliance activities, added assistance and grants for the establishment of State safety and health programs, and funds for a national survey of occupational injuries and illnesses.

The recommendation will provide for a total of approximately 1,668 employees engaged in enforcement activities in 1973, an increase of approximately 685 over the 983 positions included in the budget for fiscal year 1972.

Although providing these additional funds for enforcement activities, the committee expects that the Department will improve the training of enforcement personnel and prevent overly zealous enforcement officers from dealing with employers in an unreasonable or unfair manner.

The Committee recognizes and stresses the importance of the Occupational Safety and Health Act. Therefore, it has recommended what it considers to be the maximum amount that can be effectively spent in fiscal year 1973 considering the newness of the legislation, limitations on recruiting capability and other start-up efforts required.

With these additional funds the Committee will expect the Department to significantly increase its efforts to inform and .assist businesses in the interpretation of standards and regulations to enable employers to determine whether their workplace is in compliance or what would be required for compliance.

The Committee has received a number of complaints from small businesses concerning their inability to cope with new standards and other developments in the occupational safety and health field. It is expected that the Department will assist in every way possible so as to minimize these complaints.

Source: U.S., Congress, Senate, Committee on Appropriations, "Report on the Departments of Labor, and Health, Education, and Welfare, and Related Agencies Appropriations Bill, 1973," 92d Congress, 2d Session, Report No. 92-894, pp. 14–15.

The Committee has deleted language contained in the House bill which provides that none of the funds appropriated by this Act shall be expended to pay the salaries of any employees of the Federal Government who inspect firms employing 25 persons or less for compliance with the Occupational Safety and Health Act of 1970.

BUREAU OF LABOR STATISTICS

SALARIES AND EXPENSES

1972 funds available	$37,300,000
1973 budget estimate	45,984,000
House allowance	44,784,000
Committee recommendation	45,240,000

The Committee recommends $45,240,000, an increase of $456,000 over the House Allowance and a decrease of $744,000 from the 1973 budget estimate. This amount represents an increase of $7,940,000 over the comparable appropriation in fiscal year 1972.

The recommendation provides for 1973 pay increase costs effective in January 1972 (including an additional $456,000 inadvertently omitted from the budget estimate), the fourth increment of funding for revision of the Consumer Price Index and for other essential improvements in data collection and statistical measures of economic factors of national importance.

DEPARTMENTAL MANAGEMENT

SALARIES AND EXPENSES

1972 funds available	[1] $20,619,000
1973 budget request	[2] 25,406,000
House allowance	[2] 24,156,000
Committee recommendation	[2] 24,196,000

[1] Excludes $772,000 available from the Unemployment Trust Fund.
[2] Excludes $797,000 to be transferred from the Unemployment Trust Fund.

The Committee recommends $24,196,000, an increase of $40,000 over the House Allowance, a decrease of $1,210,000 from the budget estimate, and an increase of $3,577,000 over the comparable amount available in 1972. The Committee also recommends $797,000 to be transferred from the Unemployment Trust Fund.

The increase of $40,000 over the House Allowance is to provide two additional positions for the President's Committee on Employment of the Handicapped, increasing the funds for this activity to $890,000. These new positions are to be used to provide assistance to disabled or handicapped individuals who are also disadvantaged.

SPECIAL FOREIGN CURRENCY PROGRAM

1972 funds available	$100,000
1973 budget estimate	309,000
House allowance	100,000
Committee recommendation	309,000

The Committee recommends $309,000, an increase of $209,000 over the House Allowance and the full amount of the budget request. The House Allowance provides the same amount available in 1972, which is sufficient only to finance a series of Labor Attache Conferences.

The Committee believes that the Department can effectively use excess currencies to finance activities that assist the U.S. maritime and ship-building industries, assist U.S. export industries to expand their foreign markets and conduct training seminars abroad to develop foreign craftsmen's skills for the maintenance and servicing of U.S. products.

Document 5: Portion of a Federal Appropriations Bill*

NATIONAL MEDIATION BOARD
SALARIES AND EXPENSES

For expenses necessary for carrying out the provisions of the Railway Labor Act, as amended (45 U.S.C. 151–188), including emergency boards appointed by the President, $2,888,000.

OCCUPATIONAL SAFETY AND HEALTH REVIEW
COMMISSION
SALARIES AND EXPENSES

For expenses necessary for the Occupational Safety and Health Review Commission, $5,979,000.

RAILROAD RETIREMENT BOARD
PAYMENT FOR MILITARY SERVICE CREDITS

For payments to the railroad retirement account for military service credits under the Railroad Retirement Act, as amended (45 U.S.C. 228c–1), $21,645,000.

LIMITATIONS ON SALARIES AND EXPENSES

For expenses necessary for the Railroad Retirement Board, $19,822,000 to be derived from the railroad retirement accounts.

UNITED STATES SOLDIERS' HOME
OPERATION AND MAINTENANCE

For maintenance and operation of the United States Soldiers' Home, to be paid from the Soldiers' Home permanent fund, $11,596,000: *Provided,* That this appropriation shall not be available for the payment of hospitalization of members of the Home in United States Army hospitals at rates in excess of those prescribed by the Secretary of the Army, upon recommendations of the Board of Commissioners of the Home and the Surgeon General of the Army.

CAPITAL OUTLAY

For construction of buildings and facilities, including plans and specifications, and furnishings, to be paid from the Soldiers' Home permanent fund, $244,000, to remain available until expended.

Source: U.S., Congress, Senate, *H.R. 16654, An Act Making Appropriations for the Departments of Labor, and Health, Education, and Welfare, and Related Agencies for the Fiscal Year Ending June 30, 1973, and for Other Purposes,* 92d Congress, 2d Session, pp. 38–39.

CORPORATION FOR PUBLIC BROADCASTING

PAYMENT TO THE CORPORATION FOR PUBLIC BROADCASTING

To enable the Department of Health, Education, and Welfare to make payment to the Corporation for Public Broadcasting, as authorized by section 396(k)(1) of the Communications Act of 1934, as amended, for expenses of the Corporation, $40,000,000, to remain available until expended: *Provided,* That in addition, there is appropriated

Document 6: Portion of an Object of Expenditure Budget*

APPROPRIATION ACCOUNT NO. 530

SPENDING UNIT: Department of Banking – Bureau of Loans

PAYABLE FROM: Loan Examination and State General Fund

Appropriation Account	Actual Expenditure 1970-71	Actual Expenditure 1971-72	Appropriation 1972-73	Estimated Expenditure 1972-73	Requested by Spending Unit 1973-74	Requested by Spending Unit 1974-75	Recommended By Governor 1973-74	Recommended By Governor 1974-75
SALARIES:								
Supervisor, Bureau of Loans	(1) 14,440.00	(1) 15,712.20		(1) 15,834.00	(1) 16,523.00	(1) 17,199.00		
Loan Examiner II	(2) 19,091.00	(4) 38,789.50		(5) 51,935.00	(7) 77,896.00	(8) 89,024.00		
Loan Examiner I	(3) 22,504.00	(5) 17,027.85		(6) 55,926.00	(8) 80,288.00	(8) 80,288.00		
Clerk Stenographer III	.....	.....		(1) 6,591.00	(1) 7,878.00	(1) 7,878.00		
Clerk Stenographer II	(1) 5,623.00	(1) 6,424.30		(1) 6,877.00	(1) 6,877.00	(1) 6,877.00		
Clerk Typist I	.....	(1) 4,755.65		(1) 5,447.00	(1) 5,447.00	(1) 5,447.00		
Clerk Typist II	.....	.....		(2) 12,610.00	.....	.....		
Clerk Stenographer I	.....	(1) 2,445.15		(1) 6,019.00	(3) 18,915.00	(3) 18,915.00		
Total Salaries	(7) 61,658.00	(13) 85,154.65	260,768.00	(18) 161,239.00	(22) 213,824.00	(23) 225,628.00	213,824.00	225,628.00
OTHER EXPENSES:								
Supplies and Materials	.....	1,260.43		6,000.00	4,000.00	4,000.00		
Postage, Telephone and Telegraph	348.85	2,645.35		12,000.00	10,000.00	10,000.00		
Travel Expense	11,839.86	25,459.88		50,000.00	43,000.00	43,000.00		
Printing and Binding	32.38	881.08		3,000.00	2,000.00	2,000.00		
Motor Vehicle Operations	2,933.76	6,777.26		12,000.00	7,500.00	7,500.00		
Repairs and Alterations	38.35	67.20		5,200.00	500.00	500.00		
Insurance and Bonding	92.50	92.50		200.00	300.00	300.00		
Rental of Premises	2,496.60	2,496.60		14,396.00	10,000.00	10,000.00		
Dues	50.00	350.00		350.00	200.00	200.00		
Subscriptions	4.00	4.00		4.00	4.00	4.00		
Total Other Expenses	17,836.30	40,034.30	103,150.00	103,150.00	77,504.00	77,504.00	77,504.00	77,504.00
EQUIPMENT PURCHASES:								
Office Equipment	154.00	3,500.70	1,500.00	1,500.00	4,000.00	3,000.00	4,000.00	3,000.00
Sub-Totals	79,648.30	128,689.65	365,418.00	265,889.00	295,328.00	306,132.00	295,328.00	306,132.00
Employees Insurance	867.72	1,097.33	2,200.00	2,200.00	3,000.00	3,000.00	3,000.00	3,000.00
Employees Retirement	3,473.34	4,931.46	8,000.00	8,000.00	9,000.00	9,000.00	9,000.00	9,000.00
Social Security	2,577.65	3,180.77	8,000.00	8,000.00	9,000.00	9,000.00	9,000.00	9,000.00
GRAND TOTALS	86,567.01	137,899.21	383,618.00	284,089.00	316,328.00	327,132.00	316,328.00	327,132.00

*Source: State of Alabama, Executive Budget, State General Fund and Trust Funds for the Fiscal Years Ending September 30, 1974 and September 30, 1975, p. 189

Document 7: Portion of a Performance Budget*

GENERAL ADMINISTRATION–PATUXENT INSTITUTION

Program and Performance:

Patuxent Institution, established at Jessup, Maryland in 1954, is a maximum security institution with a physical capacity of 640 patients. An Outpatient Clinic Service and a Halfway House located in Baltimore City, provide continued treatment and support for pre-parole and paroled patients. The Institutional Board of Review and the Board of Patuxent Institution are funded under this program. Responsibility for the review of each patient and the authority to grant periodic leaves and parole to selected individual patients is vested in the Institutional Board of Review, a multidiscipline review authority established by statute. The Board of Patuxent Institution provides general consultative and advisory services on problems and matters relating to the Institution to both the staff of the Institution and the Secretary. The General Administration program provides for the executive direction and supervision of the operating departments and programs of the entire Institution. Responsibility for overall planning, development and the review of the major functions of the Institution such as confinement, diagnosis, treatment and research, as well as personnel administration, fiscal management, supply procurement and distribution, communication and related services are provided in this program.

	Actual 1974	Actual 1975	Estimated 1976	Estimated 1977
Units of Measurement:				
Average Daily Population	455	476	525	510
Admissions.	325	201	300	275
Discharges	240	205	240	250
Annual Per Capita Cost.	$11,788	$12,682	$11,501	$12,058
Daily Per Capita Cost	$ 32.30	$ 34.75	$ 31.42	$ 33.04

Source: State of Maryland, *The Maryland State Budget for the Fiscal Year Ending June 30, 1977,* Volume 2, 1976, pp. 137–138.

DEPARTMENT OF PUBLIC SAFETY AND CORRECTIONAL SERVICES

Appropriation Statement:

		1975 Actual	1976 Appropriation	1977 Allowance
	Number of Authorized Positions . . .	20	21	21
01	Salaries and Wages.	220,997	246,123	252,326
02	Technical and Special Fees	7,300	6,000	8,800
03	Communication	12,968	12,700	14,650
04	Travel	1,995	3,500	2,700
08	Contractual Services.	34,542	69,622	38,600
09	Supplies and Materials	15,133	13,350	14,000
10	Equipment—Replacement.	. . . . . .	920	570
11	Equipment—Additional	913	40	. . . . . .
13	Fixed Charges.	751	57,473	99,138
	Total Operating Expenses	66,302	157,605	169,658
	Total Expenditure.	294,599	409,728	430,784
	Original General Fund Appropriation.	293,862	398,898	
	Transfer of General Fund Appropriation.	1,457	10,830	
	Total General Fund Appropriation	295,319		
	Less: General Fund Reversion	720		
	Net General Fund Expenditure.	294,599	409,728	430,784

Budget Bill Text:
35.04.00.01 General Administration
General Fund Appropriation 430,784

Document 8: Portion of a Program Budget*

PROTECTION OF PERSONS AND PROPERTY

Subcategory: Regulation of the Insurance Industry

OBJECTIVE: To assure the efficiency of the insurance industry and its ability to satisfy contractual obligations and to prevent abuse by illegal or unfair practices.

Recommended Program Costs:

(Dollar Amounts in Thousands)

	1971–72	1972–73	1973–74	1974–75	1975–76	1976–77	1977–78
General Fund	$ 3,141	$ 3,664	$ 4,084	$ 4,331	$ 4,578	$ 4,858	$ 5,166
Other Funds	85	50	60	60	60	59	50
Total	$ 3,226	$ 3,714	$ 4,144	$ 4,391	$ 4,638	$ 4,917	$ 5,216

Program Measures:

	1971–72	1972–73	1973–74	1974–75	1975–76	1976–77	1977–78
Savings through reduction of insurance premiums (in thousands)	$135,460	$163,810	$230,310	$229,130	$237,050	$251,270	$264,460
Savings from no-fault insurance (in thousands)	.....	.....	$ 80,000	$ 84,000	$ 89,000	$ 95,000	$ 98,000
Savings from departmental intervention (in thousands)	$ 2,000	$ 2,500	$ 3,000	$ 3,400	$ 3,500	$ 3,600	$ 3,600
Medical care savings (in thousands)	$ 66,000	$ 72,000	$ 76,320	$ 80,899	$ 85,732	$ 90,250	$ 93,300

Source: Milton J. Shapp, Governor, Commonwealth of Pennsylvania, *1973-1974 Governor's Executive Budget,* Volume 2, p. 85.

Program Analysis:

This program is responsive to the changing needs of the consumer as well as the insurance industry in general. It attempts to ensure that the industry is doing everything possible to make the insurance market responsive to the needs of the consumers by making available to them reliable and responsible choices for needed insurance coverages at appropriate rates. At the same time, it tries to promote an economic climate within the industry that will allow any company operating within statutory law, to realize a reasonable rate of return on its business.

Through the series of "Shoppers' Guides" on buying various types of insurance, reforms of Blue Shield and the medical profession, a crackdown on mail order advertising, instituting consumer complaint services, publishing investors' guides, the consumer is being protected, his awareness raised and his money saved.

Total dollar savings to the consumer in Pennsylvania amounted to about $200 million during 1972–73. In rejection of premium increases for 1972, the savings amounted to $135 million. The subscribers of Blue Cross alone, realized cumulative savings of $36 million. The investigation of individual complaints against specific insurance activities brought about a savings of over $2 million and another $10 million was saved through the disclosure of various gimmick policies which have been offered to the Commonwealth's consumers.

Finally, it is estimated that if no-fault insurance becomes a reality, the Commonwealth citizenry can expect to save an additional $80 million during the first year. There should also be a secondary benefit of having more prompt payment to the victims of motor vehicle accidents through the reduction of the need to resort to lawsuits and litigation.

With the emphasis placed on the insurance industry, it would be expected that there would be an unwillingness on the part of some insurance companies to do business in the Commonwealth. On the contrary, there were no insurance firms that voluntarily refused to do business in Pennsylvania, nor are there insurance companies expected to be placed in liquidation because of bankruptcy resulting from the Commonwealth's activities.

Index